Life & Times in 20th-Century America

Volume 2: Boom Times, Hard Times

1921–1940

Greenwood Publishing Group

Library of Congress Cataloging-in-Publication Data

Life & times in 20th-century America / by Media Projects, Inc.

    p. cm

    Includes bibliographical references and indexes.

  Contents: v. 1. Becoming a modern nation, 1900-1920 — v. 2. Boom times, hard times, 1921-1940 — v. 3. Hot and cold wars, 1941-1960 — v. 4. Troubled times at home, 1961-1980 — v. 5. Promise and change, 1981-2000.

ISBN 0–313–32570–7 (set: alk. paper)—ISBN 0–313–32571–5 (v. 1: alk. paper) — ISBN 0–313–32572–3 (v. 2: alk. paper)—ISBN 0–313–32573–1 (v. 3: alk. paper) — ISBN 0–313-32574–X (v. 4: alk. paper)—ISBN 0–313–32575–8 (v. 5: alk. paper)

  1. United States—History—20th century. 2. United States—Social conditions—20th century. 3. United States—Social life and customs—20th century. I. Media Projects Incorporated.

E741.L497 2004

973.91—dc21   2003044829

British Library Cataloguing in Publication Data is available.

Library of Congress Catalog Card Number: 2003044829

ISBN: 0–313–32570–7 (set)

      0–313–32571–5 (vol. 1)

      0–313–32572–3 (vol. 2)

      0–313–32573–1 (vol. 3)

      0–313–32574–X (vol. 4)

      0–313–32575–8 (vol. 5)

First published in 2004

Greenwood Press, 88 Post Road West, Westport, CT 06881
An imprint of Greenwood Publishing Group, Inc.
www.greenwood.com

Printed in the United States of America

The paper used in this book complies with the Permanent Paper Standard issued by the National Information Standards Organization (Z39.48–1984).

10 9 8 7 6 5 4 3 2 1

Media Projects, Inc.
Managing Editor: Carter Smith
Writer: Charles A. Wills
Editor: Carolyn Jackson
Production Editor: Jim Burmester
Indexer: Marilyn Flaig
Designer: Amy Henderson
Copy Editor: Elin Woodger

Contents

Life on a Roller Coaster

In 1920, there were forty-eight stars in the U.S. flag. Alaska and Hawaii were still territories and would not become states until almost forty years later. The frontier—the dividing line between settled and unsettled land—had disappeared in 1890. Nevertheless, there were still plenty of wide-open spaces, especially in the West and Southwest. East of the Mississippi River and especially along the northern Atlantic coast, the land was more heavily populated.

One way to learn about history is through demography, the study and use of population information. According to the Census of 1920, the U.S. population was about 106.5 million, up from about 76 million in 1900. By mid-2002, it would be 287.6 million. In 1920, for the first time in American history, more Americans lived in cities and towns of more than 2,500 people than lived in rural areas.

Despite this change, America was still largely a nation of small towns. Fewer than a quarter of the population lived in cities of more than 100,000. The biggest city by far was New York City with about 5.6 million residents. The next most populous city was Chicago with 2.7 million, followed by Philadelphia with 1.8 million. The most populous cities west of the Mississippi River were Los Angeles (576,000), San Francisco (500,000), and Seattle (319,000).

By 1940, the nation's population had risen to nearly 132 million. In twenty years, the country's population had grown by more than 25 million people—a big change for two decades. What the numbers do not tell us, however is where people lived. Despite the growing population nationwide, some places, like Oklahoma and South Dakota, actually had fewer people in 1940 than twenty years earlier. More important, the population number in 1940 does not tell us how average people lived.

CLOCKWISE: **New York Yankees Lou Gehrig and Babe Ruth; A young woman shows her support for the end of Prohibition; a group of African Americans outside of a "colored only" Mississippi store.** (All photos: Library of Congress)

The Boom and Bust Decades

The years from 1920 to 1940 were among the most dramatic in U.S. history. Not since the Civil War and not again until the 1960s would life change so much for the nation and its citizens. The popular view of this era is that it was a decade of prosperity and plenty followed by a decade of depression and discouragement. This view is true in a broad sense, but the reality is more complicated.

The 1920s began with the nation's economy in a slump. It had not recovered completely from the Great War, later called World War I. That war had ended in November 1918. During the early 1920s, however, most of America's industries were more highly productive than ever. Gross National Product (the value of all the goods and services produced by a nation) rose from about $60 million in 1921 to $87 million in 1929. By 1930 the United States was producing more than one-third of the world's industrial output.

By the mid-1920s, millions of Americans working in factories, offices, and shops were earning bigger paychecks. The average yearly income went from $522 in 1921 to $716 in 1929. The standard of living rose. More and more working Americans could enjoy things their parents had only dreamed of, including an eight-hour workday, a five-day workweek, paid vacations, and even an automobile. Thanks to higher wages (and the new pay-as-you-

1921

The first Miss America beauty pageant takes place in Atlantic City, New Jersey. The first winner is sixteen-year-old Margaret Gorman.

1922

The period known as the Harlem Renaissance begins when *Harlem Shadows*, by African American writer Claude McKay, is published.

1923

Congress passes the Snyder Act, making all Native Americans citizens of the United States.

1924

Jimmy Carter becomes the first future president of the United States to be born in a hospital.

Republican Calvin Coolidge defeats Democrat John W. Davis in the presidential election.

Young adults in the "Roaring Twenties" wore new fashions, danced new dance steps, and sometimes behaved in ways that their parents disapproved of. (Library of Congress)

go credit plans) ordinary Americans could afford items that were considered luxuries just a few years before.

The 1920s were often called the "Roaring Twenties" because many parts of American life speeded up. Business and industry boomed. So did crime. When the sale of alcohol was made illegal in 1919, criminals went into business to produce and sell it. Young upper- and middle-income Americans often behaved in ways that shocked their parents. They danced in "speakeasies" where illegal drinks were sold. Women cut their hair short, wore short dresses, smoked, and told naughty jokes. Jazz, the new American music with roots in African American culture, set everyone's toes tapping.

But the Twenties did not roar for everyone. The boom left behind many Americans. Prices for farm products fell throughout the decade, causing poverty in rural areas. Job opportunities were also limited for those who were not white. Few African Americans or other minorities shared in the new prosperity.

Still, most Americans seemed to agree with Republican president

1925

The Scopes "Monkey Trial" takes place. Teacher John Scopes is convicted of breaking a state law that made it illegal to "teach any theory that denies the story of Divine Creation of man as taught in the Bible, and to teach that man is descended from a lower order of mammals."

1926

Wings, a movie about combat during World War I, featuring actors Clara Bow and Buddy Rogers, wins the first Academy Award for Best Picture.

1927

Although there is little evidence of guilt, Nicola Sacco and Bartolomeo Vanzetti are convicted of murdering two men in a robbery.

1927

Pilot Charles A. Lindbergh takes off from Roosevelt Field on Long Island, New York, in his single-engine plane, *The Spirit of St. Louis*. Thirty-three hours later, he lands in Paris, France, becoming the first man to fly across the Atlantic Ocean nonstop.

Calvin Coolidge when he said "the chief business of America is business." By the late 1920s, it appeared to many that American business and industry could meet any challenge. Despite some troubling signs—like the wild trading on the stock market—most people expected the good times to continue.

A Nation of Immigrants

America in 1920 was close to its immigrant roots. In the years between 1880 and about 1920, almost 24 million immigrants entered the United States. Close to half of all white Americans in 1920 were either foreign-born or had at least one immigrant parent.

This huge tide of immigration greatly changed the nation's ethnic makeup. Before 1880, most immigrants to the United States came from Northern Europe, especially Ireland, Germany, Great Britain, and Scandinavia. Most of the post-1880 wave of immigrants arrived from Central, Southern, and Eastern Europe—Italy, Poland, Hungary, Russia, Bohemia (now the Czech Republic), and so on. Many were Jews from Eastern Europe. By 1920, the Jewish population of New York City was more than 1.5 million.

In 1920, the term *ethnic group* was just coming into use in the United States. The Census of 1920 listed more than 106 ethnic groups. The census classified about 90 percent of Americans as white. There was no category for Americans of Hispanic origin until many years later, so the Spanish-speaking

1927

New York Yankee outfielder Babe Ruth hits a record 60 home runs. His single-season record lasts for more than 30 years.

1928

Republican Herbert Hoover defeats Democrat Alfred E. Smith in the presidential election.

1929

On a day known as "Black Tuesday," panic spreads across Wall Street as prices on the stock market plunge. Millionaires and ordinary investors lose their life savings in a matter of days. A ten-year period of hard times called the Great Depression begins.

1930

In response to the Great Depression, the U.S. Congress passes the Smoot-Hawley Act. The law dramatically raises tariffs, or taxes on imported goods. The new law leads to European countries raising tariffs on goods coming from the United States.

population in 1920 is not known. However, it was growing. About 500,000 Mexicans emigrated to the southwestern states between 1910 and 1920, a time of civil war and revolution in Mexico.

As the 1920s began, many Americans decided that it had been a mistake to get involved in the Great War. They began to urge the United States to stay out of world affairs. This movement was called *isolationism*. Its followers, called isolationists, had led the Senate to reject the international League of Nations that President Woodrow Wilson had proposed at the end of the war. Now isolationists urged new immigration laws. These new laws greatly reduced immigration from Southern and Eastern Europe and nearly excluded Asians. They gave preference to immigrants from Northern Europe and the Americas.

A Return to Normalcy

To better understand how American life developed in the 1920s and 1930s, it is helpful to explore the lives and legacies of the four men who served as president during the era.

The presidential election of 1920 was the first in which women could vote. In August 1920, the Nineteenth Amendment to the U.S. Constitution achieved ratification (approval) by the required number of states and became law. It had taken more than seventy years of determined effort—starting with the first organized women's rights conference, at Seneca Falls, New York, in

1931
Treasury Department agents gather enough evidence to send Chicago gangster Al Capone to prison for tax evasion.

1932
One thousand soldiers and six tanks break up a camp of World War I veterans left jobless by the Depression. Nick-named the "Bonus Army," the veterans had asked that money the government promised to pay them in 1945 be paid in advance.

1932
Democrat Franklin Delano Roosevelt defeats Republican president Herbert Hoover in the presidential election.

1932
At the Olympic Games, American athlete Babe Didrickson wins the javelin throw and also sets a new women's world record of 11.7 seconds for the 80-meter hurdles.

1848—to extend the right to vote to Americans regardless of sex.

In 1920, both parties selected men from Ohio as their candidates. The Democrats nominated James M. Cox, a former governor. Cox pledged himself to continue the progressive policies of President Wilson. Cox's running mate was Franklin Delano Roosevelt. The young New Yorker had served as Assistant Secretary of the Navy in Wilson's administration.

After much debate, the Republicans settled on Senator Warren G. Harding, a small-town newspaper owner and businessman. Massachusetts governor Calvin Coolidge was his running mate.

Harding's senate career was not outstanding, and he was not a good speaker. However, he was handsome and friendly. He and the Republicans understood the public mood. People worried about the lingering effects of the

A poster promoting a woman's right to vote. (Library of Congress)

1933
Congress passes President Roosevelt's "New Deal" program, creating a number of new federal agencies aimed at ending the Depression.

1934
Actress Shirley Temple makes her movie debut at age six in *Stand Up and Cheer*. Over the next four years, she will star in six more films and become the top box-office draw in America.

1935
Dust storms in western states stop traffic along highways, close down schools, and darken daytime skies.

1935
Congress passes the Social Security Act, a program meant to protect Americans who are unable to support themselves. The act includes a plan in which money is set aside from each worker's paycheck, and payments are made to the worker after retirement.

Great War. They were also concerned about labor troubles, radical revolutionaries who might have immigrated from Europe, and the economic slump.

Candidate Harding appealed to this mood perfectly in a famous speech in May 1920. America, he said, needed "not heroics but healing; not nostrums [quick cures] but normalcy; not revolution but restoration; . . . not surgery but serenity." On election day, Harding and Coolidge easily beat Cox and Roosevelt with 60 percent of the popular vote.

Having campaigned on a promise of "less government in business and more business in government," Harding cut taxes, got rid of wartime price controls and other regulations, and set up a federal Bureau of the Budget to monitor government spending. These measures seemed to work. By 1923, the great boom had begun.

Harding's administration was conservative economically but liberal in other areas. For example, the new president freed from prison accused radicals, including the socialist leader Eugene V. Debs, who opposed most private enterprise. Harding also appointed many capable individuals to his cabinet. Herbert Hoover served as Secretary of Commerce and Andrew Mellon as Secretary of the Treasury.

President Warren Harding
(Library of Congress)

Still, history has not been kind to Harding. Fairly or unfairly, his presidency is remembered most-

1936

Democratic president Franklin Roosevelt wins reelection, defeating Republican challenger Alfred Landon.

1937

President Roosevelt proposes that the president be allowed to appoint a new Supreme Court justice each time a member of the Supreme Court reaches seventy years old and does not retire. Roosevelt's plan fails to win approval from the Senate.

1939

Novelist John Steinbeck's book The Grapes of Wrath is published. The book tells the story of a family of migrant workers who leave Oklahoma in search of work in California.

1940

Franklin Delano Roosevelt defeats Wendell Willkie to win a third term as president.

ly for its corruption and scandals. Harding himself was honest, but he surrounded himself with corrupt friends who came to be called the Ohio Gang. Harding appointed some of its members to high office, with disastrous results. Charles Forbes, director of the Veterans Bureau, and his associates looted millions of dollars meant for veterans' medical care. Harry Daughtery, who had been Harding's campaign manager, became attorney general. He also appeared more interested in building up his bank account than serving the public.

The most famous scandal of the era, however, did not involve the Ohio Gang but Albert Fall of New Mexico. Fall was Harding's Secretary of the Interior. He was found guilty of leasing the Teapot Dome oil preserve in Wyoming to private companies in return for bribes. Fall became the first cabinet member in U.S. history to wind up behind prison bars.

Although Harding was not personally involved in the scandal, he did know about it and decided to keep it a secret. Returning from a trip to Alaska, Harding died of a heart attack in San Francisco on August 2, 1923. Some felt the strain caused by the scandal had contributed to his collapse. In April 1924, the Senate at last began its investigation of what came to be known as the "Teapot Dome scandal."

Calvin Coolidge: Keeping Cool

News of Harding's death reached Plymouth Notch, Vermont, where Vice President Calvin Coolidge was visiting with his family, early on the morning of August 3. By the flickering light of a kerosene lamp, Coolidge's father, a judge, swore in his son as the nation's twenty-ninth president.

Like Harding, Coolidge appeared to embody the virtues of small-town America. But Harding was a sociable man, fond of a game of poker and a glass of whiskey. Coolidge could seem as stern as the rocky hills of his native New England.

Coolidge first won nationwide attention as governor of Massachusetts. When the Boston police force went on strike in 1919, Coolidge sent a telegram to the great labor leader Samuel Gompers, stating his belief that "There is no right to strike against the public safety by anybody, anywhere, any time."

Calvin Coolidge
(Library of Congress)

That statement (and Coolidge's handling of the strike, which ended with all the strikers being fired) had convinced Republican leaders that Coolidge was the ideal running mate for Harding.

Coolidge was elected president in his own right in 1924. He ran under the slogan "Keep Cool with Coolidge." With former Bureau of the Budget director Charles G. Dawes as his running mate, he had no trouble beating both Democrat John W. Davis and Progressive Robert LaFollette.

The Coolidge administration is remembered for little change in government policies. Coolidge reflected the contentment many Americans felt as wages rose and the stock market set record highs. This situation suited Coolidge's hands-off style perfectly.

Coolidge could almost certainly have won a second term. However, in August 1927, he called a press conference and announced, "I do not choose to run for president in 1928."

Historians have long debated why Coolidge did not run again. Did he see the Great Depression looming ahead? Possibly. Even though he famously said that "the chief business of America is business," Coolidge may have sensed that the boom would not last forever. In January 1928, trading on the New York Stock Exchange soared when Coolidge said he did not see anything wrong with investors using borrowed money to buy shares. This is a practice known as "speculation."

Six months later, however, Coolidge noted, "Prosperity is only an instrument to be used, not a deity [a god] to be worshipped." This seemed to be a comment on both the wild trading in stocks and the general get-rich-quick atmosphere of the boom years.

Herbert Hoover: The Great Engineer

The election of 1928 showed the political and social conflicts that lay beneath the surface of the general prosperity. On the surface, the election was between Republican Herbert Hoover and Democrat Al Smith. But many people saw it as a contest between different views of America. It pitted the small town against the big city. It was a contest between those whose families had lived in the United States for generations and the children of recent immigrants. Some believed success or failure was up to the individual. Others believed the government had a duty to help those in need. It also pitted "drys," who favored the continued prohibition of alcohol, against a growing number of "wets," who opposed Prohibition because of the crime that it brought.

Hoover had been Secretary of Commerce under both Harding and Coolidge. Born on an Iowa farm to Quaker parents, he was orphaned at an early age and raised by relatives. After graduating from Stanford University, Hoover worked as a mining engineer in many remote and dangerous places

around the world. He became respected and wealthy in the process.

During and after World War I, Hoover managed American relief efforts in Europe and Russia. He made sure that food and medicine reached millions of starving and suffering people. This won him a reputation as both a great humanitarian and a brilliant administrator. Some called him the Great Engineer. Personally, he was quiet, serious, and a compulsive worker.

Herbert Hoover
(Library of Congress)

Democrat Alfred E. Smith, universally known as Al, could not have been more different from Hoover. As a grandson of Irish immigrants, Smith grew up on New York's Lower East Side; "The Sidewalks of New York" was his campaign song. He rose through the ranks of Tammany Hall, New York's Democratic Party machine (so called because it provided votes with machine-like precision). He had served three terms as governor of New York, beginning in 1918.

Smith was sunny. His nickname, the "Happy Warrior," fit him like his trademark brown derby hat. He was also a Roman Catholic, the first Catholic to win a major party's presidential nomination. In 1928, Smith's faith was a major issue for some Protestant Americans who believed that Catholics could never be true Americans because of their supposed allegiance to the Pope.

In the end, the booming economy probably played a bigger role in the outcome of the election than Smith's background, religion, or opposition to

Prohibition. The Republicans claimed responsibility for the prosperous economy. Their motto was "a chicken in every pot and a car in every garage." On Election Day, Hoover won all but eight states. He even beat Smith in New York State.

Seven months after Hoover took office, the good times came to a sudden end. On October 24, 1929—a day known ever after as Black Thursday—share prices on the New York Stock Exchange took a huge fall. For a few days, it seemed like the market might recover, but on October 29 (Black Tuesday), the market fell even further. Three days after Black Tuesday, the president went on the radio to state his belief that "the fundamental business of the country . . . is on a sound and prosperous basis." It was a note he repeated in May 1930, when he said, "We shall rapidly recover." Instead, things got worse. The stage was now set for the Great Depression—the worst peacetime crisis ever endured by the American people.

The Great Depression

The Crash of 1929 was not the only cause of the Great Depression. Countries around the world had economic problems of their own. For example, Germany was still struggling to pay its huge debts from the Great War. This affected Germany's trade with other countries in Europe and the United States.

Even so, in the days and months that followed Black Tuesday, many Americans kept their faith in Hoover's ability to deal with the crisis. After all, the Great Engineer had seemingly worked miracles before.

Hoover took some steps to halt bank failures, factory closings, and layoffs. In late 1931, for example, he called on Congress to set up the Reconstruction Finance Corporation (RFC) to provide loans to businesses, farms, and banks in danger of going under. He also approved a limited program of public works to create jobs.

By the turn of the decade, though, America's economy was in a downward spiral. National income had almost doubled in the 1920s, but it fell by more than half between 1929 and 1933. Many people stopped buying anything but essentials like food. With demand for consumer products dropping, some employers cut wages for workers. Salaries fell by 40 percent during these years. Even with deep pay cuts, workers who had jobs considered themselves lucky. By the end of 1932, about 14 million Americans were out of work.

Only a few years before, many families had been thinking about buying a new car or radio. Now they worried about paying their rent or installments on loans they had taken out to buy a home. Some had lost their homes altogether. Perhaps a million Americans were already homeless by 1933. Many worried about their next meal.

Hoover's position was that government should not become deeply involved in the economy. He also opposed, at first, direct government relief for the unemployed. The president maintained that relief went against the American tradition of self-reliance.

Millions of jobless, hungry, and homeless Americans had a hard time understanding their president's attitude. Hoover had won worldwide respect by administering relief to war-ravaged Europeans. Now he seemed unwilling to give the same help to depression-ravaged Americans.

People were understandably bitter, and they took this bitterness out on the president. Every town and city seemed to have its cluster of cardboard and scrap-lumber shacks sheltering the homeless. These settlements became known as "Hoovervilles."

The low point for Hoover came in the summer of the election year of 1932. In 1924, Congress had passed a law granting a cash bonus to veterans of the Great War. It was to be paid in 1945. The depression, however, led to a movement among veterans for early payment of the bonus.

During May 1932, about 20,000 veterans and families arrived in Washington, D.C. Camping in parks, vacant lots, and empty buildings, bonus demonstrators pledged to stay until Congress authorized early payment. An early-payment bill passed the House of Representatives but was defeated in the Senate. (Hoover opposed the bill, because early payment would have cost more than $2 billion, or 25 percent of the entire federal budget.)

With the bill's defeat, most of the so-called Bonus Army left Washington. By late July, just a few thousand veterans and their families remained. Their good relations with police turned sour after policemen killed two veterans in a scuffle. Hoover ordered the army to help the police shut down the veterans' camp in the Anacostia Flats area. Muddled communica-

During the Great Depression, many Americans, like these children, lived in slum areas made of no more than wooden shacks. Because many people blamed President Herbert Hoover for not doing more to revive the economy, these slums were often called "Hoovervilles." (Library of Congress)

tions and the high-handed actions of the army's chief of staff, Major General Douglas MacArthur, made the operation a disaster.

The army used tanks, tear gas, and bayonets to clear the veteran's camp, which caught fire. The number of people injured and killed—or even whether anyone actually died—is still unclear. However, what became known as the Battle of Anacostia Flats was a tragedy for the nation and a public-relations nightmare for Hoover.

Hoover won the Republican Party's nomination in the presidential election of 1932, but he lost the election to Democratic candidate Franklin Delano Roosevelt by 8 million votes.

The Dust Bowl

Hunger and hopelessness were part of life everywhere. The Depression drove crop prices down even further. Nature itself seemed to be turning against

A dust storm blows through a small Oklahoma town. (Library of Congress)

the nation's farmers. A period of drought began in 1930. The lack of rain ruined crops across the Midwest and Great Plains. Soon massive dust storms whipped up dried topsoil to create what would be known as the "dust bowl." The dust bowl stretched north as far as South Dakota, Wyoming, and Nebraska, through Kansas and Colorado to Oklahoma, Texas, and New Mexico. It affected states as far east as Kentucky, as far north as the Dakotas, and as far west as Nevada. More than 3 million people fled the dust bowl in the 1930s.

FDR Cheers a Nation

On March 4, 1933, Franklin Delano Roosevelt took the oath of office as president. Millions of Americans listened to his inaugural address on their radios. His memorable words included, "Let me assert my firm belief that the only thing we have to fear is fear itself...." He ended the speech by asking Congress for "broad executive power" to fight the Depression. The power he asked for was "as great as the power that would be given to me if we were... invaded by a foreign foe."

Roosevelt's words of reassurance and his determination to act gave heart to a discouraged nation. Even so, few that day could have foreseen that the new president would remain in the White House for twelve of the most challenging years of American history. During that time, he would forever change the role government plays in the lives of Americans.

Franklin D. Roosevelt was born in 1882 to a prominent New York family. After attending Harvard, he worked as a lawyer. Then he went into politics, winning election to the New York State legislature from his home district in the Hudson River Valley.

Roosevelt contracted polio, a sometimes fatal disease caused by a virus, in 1921, while vacationing in Canada with his family. He would spend the rest of his life in a wheelchair. Although unable to walk without help and metal braces to steady his legs, he never let voters see that he could not stand alone.

Roosevelt returned to politics in 1924 by making a stirring speech at the Democratic National Convention. Four years later, he succeeded Al Smith as governor of New York. In 1933, he was elected president and served until his death in 1945.

The New Deal

President Roosevelt, who was often called FDR, was popular with working people. Although personally rich, his fight with polio gave him strong sympathy for the underdog and an understanding of what it was like to struggle against difficult circumstances. He gave people hope.

FDR had campaigned on the promise of "a new deal for the American people." Roosevelt proposed federal programs that would promote economic recovery by offering people better opportunity, a fresh start, like a "new deal" in a game of cards.

Roosevelt took office in 1933 for what would be the first of four terms in office. In the first hundred days of his administration, Congress passed a sweeping series of laws that put his New Deal into practice (see Chapter 5). Federal funds became available for relief (called welfare today) for the jobless. The new laws promoted agricultural development. They also put the unemployed to work building public-works projects such as dams, bridges, roads, and housing.

More controversially, the federal government began to regulate parts of the economy and to protect the rights of labor unions. Many businesspeople objected that government should not get involved with private enterprise, but Roosevelt persisted. In 1935, the president signed the Social Security Act, which provides aid to people 65 and older and to disabled and unemployed workers. The 1938 Fair Labor Standards Act established the first minimum wage—forty cents an hour. The act also set the workweek at forty hours. It was the last piece of New Deal legislation.

The New Deal did much to ease the suffering of individual Americans. It also helped to restore the confidence of millions of Americans in democracy and free enterprise. However, the New Deal did not bring back the prosperity of the 1920s. Throughout the 1930s, many people struggled to keep food on their table and a roof over their heads. In the mid-1930s, the jobless rate finally began to fall, although it stalled again in 1936. Not until 1940–1941 did employment rates and industrial production approach their 1929 levels.

Franklin Delano Roosevelt
(Library of Congress)

A Very Powerful President

Like any president, Roosevelt had his critics. To some on the political left, he did not go far enough in regulating business and establishing social welfare programs. To some on the right, he was a dangerous radical who wanted to do away with free enterprise and run everyone's life from Washington.

Critics on both sides occasionally accused him of acting like a dictator. In truth, he liked to have his way. After the Supreme Court ruled the Agriculture Adjustment Act and the National Industrial Recovery Act unconstitutional, he decided to change the court. In 1937, he tried to "pack" the Supreme Court by appointing additional justices who favored New Deal programs. However, he did not succeed.

Unlike the dictators, such as Adolf Hitler and Joseph Stalin, who brought misery to so much of the world in the 1930s, Roosevelt was not motivated by a lust for personal power. Neither did he have a strong political philosophy. He described his political style as, "Take a method and try it.

If it fails, admit it frankly and try another. But above all, try something."

Roosevelt's goals were to get the country on its feet again and provide help to those who really needed it. He was a master of compromise and a genius at bringing different groups together. Through it all, Roosevelt worked within the democratic system to get what he wanted.

Almost 70 years after his first inaugural, Franklin Roosevelt's legacy is still with us, in things like Social Security, stock-market regulations, and the minimum wage. No less a conservative than President Ronald Reagan (a New Deal supporter as a young man) often praised FDR for his great leadership in difficult times. And a recent poll of American historians placed Franklin Roosevelt third in a ranking of great presidents—behind only George Washington and Abraham Lincoln.

World War II Begins in Europe

Although the New Deal gave millions new hope, it failed to end the Great Depression. Instead, it was World War II that gave the economy the boost it needed. Like the Great War, it began in Europe—in September 1939. The United States would not enter the war until Germany's ally, Japan, attacked Pearl Harbor, Hawaii, in December 1941. But as 1940 ended, President Roosevelt called on the nation to become "the great arsenal of democracy." This meant building up America's defenses and providing aid to Great Britain and the Soviet Union, who were already fighting Nazi Germany. (In 1922, Communist Russia had formed a union with five neighboring countries to create the more powerful Union of Soviet Socialist Republics. The larger nation was called the Soviet Union for short.)

In order to produce supplies for America's allies in Europe, U.S. factories that had been shut down for a decade now began to operate twenty-four hours a day. They turned out tanks and planes and the million other items needed for modern warfare. After twenty hard years, farmers received higher prices for their crops. Within a few years, there was a good-paying job for anyone who was not in the armed services.

As the United States entered World War II, its strength and resolve would be greatly tested. Yet it was able to do so more confidently and with greater strength than when it had entered World War I. The years of boom and bust

Chapter One

Family Life

Photographer Dorothea Lange took this famous photograph (LEFT) of a worried 32-year-old mother of seven in a California migrant worker camp in 1936. Members of the Wilkins family (RIGHT) are at dinner on corn-shucking day in Salem, North Carolina. (Library of Congress)

The lives of American families varied widely in the 1920s and 1930s, just as they do in our own time. Family life on a sprawling Midwestern farm, for example, was very different from family life in a crowded neighborhood in a big East Coast city. Nevertheless, American family life had certain common characteristics.

Regardless of where they lived and how they made their livings, most Americans lived in a family setting. Marriage and child raising were the normal pattern for people who grew up during this time. About three out of five adults lived as part of a married couple. The average family size was four. The number of children had been dropping steadily as the nation became more urban.

Most people married young, by today's standards. The average age at first marriage in the 1920s was about twenty-five for men and twenty-one for women. The average age at marriage rose a bit during the Great Depression. Tough economic times made it harder for young couples to set up their own households.

Attitudes about Family Life

American society changed greatly between 1920 and 1930, but it was still traditional in many ways. In most places, strong religious and social pressures enforced conventional patterns of family life. Couples who lived together without being married, women who had children "out of wedlock," and married couples who divorced were often seen as bringing shame on their families.

Divorce laws had become strict at the beginning of the century. They usually required evidence of a spouse's unfaithfulness or desertion. Couples who were unhappily married for other reasons were expected to stay together.

In the mid-1920s, however, the concept of "companionate marriage" began to gain acceptance. It came to public notice in a 1925 book, *Revolt of Modern Youth*, by Juvenile Court Judge Ben B. Lindsay and Wainright Evans. The authors asserted that love and trust between husband and wife were important to married life. The concept of companionate marriage led some people to adopt a more tolerant attitude toward divorce. If marriage partners were no longer loving or trusting, some people questioned whether they should be forced to remain together. This influenced reform of divorce laws in some states to include more grounds, or reasons, for divorce.

Rates of divorce rose slightly during the 1920s. Compared to our own time, however, divorce was rare. Today about 10 percent of American adults are divorced, compared to about 1 percent in the early 1920s. The divorce rate fell sharply in the Depression years of the 1930s. Some couples couldn't afford the legal costs of divorce. Others stayed together in unhappy marriages out of economic necessity.

New Roles for Women

Attitudes about the role of women in society also changed during the 1920s and 1930s. Until the Great War (World War I, 1914–1918) most women were limited to teaching, factory and shop work, and domestic service as a cook or maid. Working women were usually expected to quit after they got married. Then they stayed home to care for children and their own household.

During the war, women entered the workforce in greater numbers. After the war, they gained the vote, and other measures of legal and political equality. Slowly a greater variety of jobs became open to them. People began to accept the idea that a woman could pursue a career separate from her role as a wife and mother. Those who did not take paid jobs were often active in the many women-only organizations.

Women shed the heavy, cumbersome clothing of their mothers' generation. Skirts no longer brushed the ground; indeed, some rose above the knees. A typical woman's dress in 1928 had seven yards of cloth, compared with nineteen yards at the beginning of the century. Hair cut short into a "bob" came into fashion. Heavy cotton or wool stockings gave way to those of sheer silk.

By 1930, more than 10 million American women worked outside the home. About 2 million worked in offices, and a similar number worked in factories. More than a million were professionals—nurses, doctors, teachers, lawyers, businesspeople, writers, artists, and so on. The percentages of women working outside the home and in the professions were far lower than they are today. Nevertheless, this represented a big advance in opportunities for women over previous decades. Although many women continued to leave the workplace after marriage, the prosperity and technical advances of the 1920s made their lives different from those of their mothers and grandmothers.

During the 1920s, the automotive industry began to advertise to women. This advertisement is aimed at the professional "woman in business." Others highlighted the usefulness of the car in doing household errands. (Library of Congress)

For the middle-class households who could afford them, new electrical appliances—especially vacuum cleaners and washing machines—took a lot of the drudgery out of housework. The growing use of prepared, prepackaged foods meant less time in the kitchen. The automobile also changed women's lives: The family car made shopping and running errands easier and helped free many housebound women.

In 1931, writer Mary Ross described how American women's lives had changed over the previous decade. "They raise their children—one, two, occasionally three or four of them—with a care probably unknown to previous generations. It is they who founded the great culture-club movement... they who spend the great American income, sustain the movie industry, buy or borrow the novels, support the fashions.... Out of this sudden burst of female leisure have come many good things."

Did appliances, cars, and the like really give American women more free time? Most 1920s and 1930s housewives still spent between 50 and 60 hours a week on housework. Families quickly came to expect cleaner clothes, tidier homes, and more varied and better-prepared meals than before. The benefits of "labor-saving" technology were often canceled out by these higher standards.

Life for Older Americans

With average life expectancy at fifty-six years for men and fifty-eight years for women, less than one American in twenty was aged sixty-five years or older in 1920. Life expectancy rose between 1920 and 1940, even in the Great Depression years. This was largely a result of better medical care.

By 1940, life expectancy stood at about sixty-eight for men and about seventy-one for women. However, life expectancy for poorer Americans—especially African Americans—lagged behind the average. In 1940, the average life expectancy for white women was about five years greater than for African American women. The figure for white men was a full fifteen years more than for African American men.

Especially during the Depression, poverty among the elderly became a problem. During the 1920s and 1930s, relatively few employers offered pensions to live on after retirement. Many were not able to save enough money to leave the workforce when they got old. In an era when most men were their family's chief bread-winner, a husband's death could mean poverty for his widow. By 1940, about 13 percent of American women were widows.

Many senior citizens (a term that came into use in 1938) lived with their adult children or other relatives. They often helped to care for young children and shared household chores. Senior citizens without family support, however, usually had to rely on charity, either public or private.

In cities, immigrant communities sometimes supported their elderly members through local organizations. In many places, however, the poorest old people had to live in bleak "almshouses" or "poor farms." Food and medical care in these places tended to be meager.

In 1935, as a part of Franklin Roosevelt's New Deal, Congress passed the Social Security Act. It provided support for some of the poorest Americans, including senior citizens. The act also provided a system of retirement insurance for workers. Employees paid into the system through money taken out of their paychecks. They would receive regular payments of an average of $22.60 per month after retiring at age 65. Social Security didn't cover all workers, however, and the first payments were not made until 1940. After that, Social Security improved the quality of life for many retired Americans.

A Nation on Wheels

Two things worked great changes in home life for American families in the 1920s and 1930s—the automobile and electricity.

Automobiles first appeared on the nation's roads and streets in large numbers in the 1890s and early 1900s. During this era, however, cars were mostly toys for the rich. Most early "horseless carriages" were expensive, complicated, and difficult to maintain.

Then a Detroit carmaker, Henry Ford, announced his plan to "...build a motor car for the great multitude. It will be large enough for the family but small enough for the individual to run and care for.... But it will be so low in price that no man making a good salary will be unable to own one, and enjoy with his family the blessings of hours and pleasure in God's great open spaces."

On October 1, 1908, the first of Ford's more than 15 million Model T Fords rolled out of the factory. The early Model Ts were basic. The boxy, 20-horsepower car started with a hand crank and came without a windshield. According to a popular story, Henry Ford told buyers that they could get their T in any color they wanted, "as long as it was black."

The first T cost $950. It got cheaper as Ford came up with ways of making cars faster and in ever-greater numbers. By the late 1920s perhaps half the cars on America's roads were Model Ts of one kind or another. A new one sold for $280. Ford replaced it with the Model A in 1927.

By the late 1920s, the "Tin Lizzie" or "Flivver," as it was nicknamed, had competition from other affordable automobiles, especially those made by Walter Durant's General Motors Corporation. Car ownership had tripled during the decade. By the beginning of the 1930s, 80 percent of American families owned at least one car. In a single generation, the United States had become a nation on wheels.

The arrival of the automobile age transformed the country in many ways. The car gave American families more freedom of movement than earlier generations could have imagined. People no longer had to live close to where they worked. Workers could now drive to offices and factories many miles from their homes or to a station where they could board a train for a nearby city. This new mobility led to a big growth in suburbs—residential communities outside the crowded neighborhoods of the big cities. This shift from city to suburb would continue for many decades.

In this 1931 photograph, a Ford salesman points out the benefits of a four-door Model A to a customer. Americans bought over four and a half million Model As beween late 1927 and the end of 1931. (Ford Motor Company News Department)

The car also changed how families spent their leisure time. In the boom years of the 1920s, many Americans enjoyed their first paid vacations. Families took to the road to visit distant cities or to enjoy the great open spaces.

Journeys in these early days of "motor tourism" were often made on dusty or muddy roads. Sometimes roads were rough enough to crack an axle even on a sturdy Model T. At the start of the 1920s, there were only 36,000 miles of paved roads outside the nation's cities. One observer noted that America's roads were "more like those of Siberia than those of France or England."

More cars created a need for more—and better—roads. Recognizing this in 1921, the federal government began to provide funds to the states to upgrade their roads. Every year, 10,000 miles of paved, all-weather roads were added to the nation's highway network.

Only one road, the Lincoln Highway (opened in 1913), stretched coast-to-coast. Most of it was unpaved in the mid-1920s. In 1925, another Federal Highway Act led to the building of numbered "interstate" highways. The showpiece of this system, the famous Route 66, was laid out a year later. By 1938, Route 66 was paved all the way from Chicago to Los Angeles.

Even with better roads, long car trips could test a family's ability to "rough it." Stopping for the night often meant pitching a tent in a field or renting rooms in a stranger's house. In the early 1920s, roadside "tourist camps" began to spring up. Most offered small cabins and shared washing and cooking facilities. These were soon joined by "motor courts" or "motor hotels" (quickly shortened to "motels"), which offered a bit more comfort and privacy.

Americans who lived in the country were even more likely to own cars than those living in the city or suburbs. Despite the slump in the rural economy that came after the Great War, farm families bought cars. The car connected them with their neighbors and community, reducing the loneliness and isolation of rural life. A family's nearest neighbors might be miles away. By horse-drawn wagon, a shopping trip to the closest town might take all day. By car, the same journey might take only an hour or two.

Electrifying America

Like the automobile, electrical power was nothing new at the start of the 1920s. Electricity had been used to light streets and power trains and factories for several decades. Electricity for lighting and for powering appliances in the home became available in many American cities from the 1880s onward.

However, just as cars were a luxury before the Model T, household electricity did not reach a majority of Americans until after the Great War. About the time that Henry Ford introduced the Model T, power-generating companies around the nation settled on a standard service. They agreed to provide 120 volts of alternating current (AC) rather than the direct current (DC) that was common in the early days of electrification. Alternating current was cheaper to produce and could be sent over greater distances. By the end of the 1920s, about 85 percent of American households were wired for electricity.

Electricity was most commonly used for lighting. People could now choose their schedules instead of arranging their lives around the hours of daylight. Before, people in cities and large towns had relied on coal gas for artificial light. However, it was not as effective as electricity in turning night into day. Electric light allowed people to work and play early in the morning or late into the night. This increased the nation's economic productivity and gave people a wider choice of leisure activities.

With electricity came an ever-wider variety of electrically powered appliances. These included irons, toasters, fans, clocks, vacuum cleaners, washing machines, and hair curlers. Electric refrigerators took longer to gain acceptance; early models were too expensive, too noisy, and too prone to mechanical breakdown for most people. In 1940, half of all American households still kept their food fresh in iceboxes, chilled by a block of ice.

American families were most enthusiastic about the radio. Between 1920—the year U.S. commercial radio broadcasts began—and 1940, they bought about 40 million radios. The radio became as central to life inside the home as the car was to life outside of it. (And cars began to get radios, too, starting in 1928.)

Outside towns and cities, however, millions of households still relied on candles and oil lamps for light. It was more expensive to generate and transmit power in rural areas. Many farm families couldn't afford electricity even when it was available. In the late 1920s, less than 10 percent of America's 6.5 million farm families had electricity.

Even before the Great Depression set in, the gap in electrification between the cities and the countryside had become a big issue for America's rural families. In 1935, the Roosevelt administration responded by setting up the Rural Electrification Administration (REA).

The REA provided federal funds to help spread power lines into areas where private power-generating companies couldn't or wouldn't operate. Thanks in large part to the REA, the number of farm families with electricity doubled between 1937 and 1940. Even so, only about 40 percent of rural households had electricity as the 1940s began.

An early advertisement (ABOVE) for the convenience of electric refrigerators. Before refrigerators were electric, people needed a constant supply of ice to keep their food fresh. A rural family (LEFT) gathers around the radio to hear a broadcast.
(Library of Congress)

A Frank Lloyd Wright–designed home in Oak Park, Illinois. (Library of Congress)

New Home Styles

The prosperous 1920s saw a big rise in home ownership. Buying a house rather than renting one was out of the reach of most American families in earlier decades. By the mid-1920s, though, a little less than half of all families owned their own homes. That percentage would drop sharply in the Great Depression, when many families could not keep up mortgage payments. Banks who had loaned the mortgages took over homes when the owners could no longer pay.

In the 1800s, American home styles had been mostly copied from European designs. They usually had several stories and lots of small, dark rooms crammed with heavy furniture. American houses changed, inside and out, during the 1920s and 1930s.

Starting in the 1890s, several architects had begun a movement toward a more American style of house. In the forefront of this movement was Frank Lloyd Wright. Wright grew up in Wisconsin and spent his early career in Chicago and it suburbs. He believed that a house should reflect the landscape on which it was built. His early designs were usually long, single-story structures with wide, overhanging roofs. Because they echoed the flat landscape of the Midwestern prairies, the homes built by Wright and architects who shared his style became known as "prairie houses." Inside, Wright's houses featured open living spaces that flowed together, usually centering on a fireplace. Lots of windows brought in light and outside views.

Only a handful of wealthy people could afford a Wright-designed house. Still, Wright influenced many architects, especially in the 1930s, when he enjoyed a new burst of popularity.

A more common house style of the 1920s and 1930s was the bungalow. Its style was adapted from traditional houses in India and popularized by the architect and furniture-maker Gustave Stickley. Bungalows were usually small—one or one-and-a-half stories tall. Inside, the space was carefully designed. Much of the furniture was built in. Bungalows were especially popular in California, where the climate favored their open, airy layout.

Because they were simple in design and inexpensive to build,

bungalows became very popular among people with modest incomes. Customers could even order bungalow-style houses in kit form from mail-order companies like Sears, Roebuck. Sears sold about 100,000 bungalow kits between 1908 and 1940.

At the end of the 1920s, a period of great economic growth, America's taste in houses returned to more old-fashioned styles. The most popular houses of the late 1920s and early 1930s were based on houses from earlier historical periods, like American Colonial or English Tudor.

By the mid-1930s, though, the Great Depression was making it difficult to build any kind of house. Wright tried to meet the challenge with his Usonian (from United States of North America) houses. These were simple houses that could be built by the owner from premade components. It was an interesting concept, but it didn't catch on.

Bungalow-style homes were very popular during the early twentieth century. These affordable homes could be built from kits purchased from mail-order companies. The bungalows seen here are located in Montour, Idaho (LEFT) and Altoona, Pennsylvania (RIGHT). (Library of Congress)

Families and the Great Depression

The lean years of the 1930s had a great impact on American family life. One effect of hard times was a steep drop in the American birthrate.

Often hard-pressed to feed and clothe the children they already had, many parents decided not to have more. Many newly married couples postponed having children at all until better times arrived. The U.S. population grew by only about 7 percent in the 1930s—about half the growth rate of the 1920s and the 1940s.

The depression broke up some families—sometimes temporarily, often permanently. Husbands and fathers in search of jobs might move to cities hundreds or thousands of miles away. They hoped to send money back their families. But with jobs scarce, many of them simply vanished. Scores of jobless men walked the highways and rode the freight trains from town to town in search of work. Teenage boys and (less frequently) girls might leave home to reduce the number of mouths their parents had to feed.

All too often, entire families wound up homeless when jobs ended and there was no money for the rent or the mortgage. Some families moved in with better-off friends or relatives. The only other available shelter might be a shack of scrap lumber and cardboard in a vacant lot or park. In the worst years of the Depression, every sizeable American community had such a "Hooverville." The makeshift quarters were named for Herbert Hoover, the president that many Americans felt had failed them.

Many farm families had already struggled through a decade or more of hard times before the Great Depression. For them, the Depression packed a double punch. Not only did crop prices fall even farther, but nature itself seemed to turn against them.

Starting in 1932, seven years of drought gripped a large area of the Midwest and Southwest, from Nebraska to Texas. As rainfall dropped off, the region's topsoil—already thinned by decades of farming—dried up and blew away. Heavy winds turned the region into a "dust bowl." Massive dust storms sometimes blotted out the midday sun. They carried hundreds of millions of tons of soil. By the end of the decade, about 10 million acres of cropland had turned to wasteland.

With their farms ruined, more than 3 million people fled the dust bowl. Many families packed all their belongings into a truck or car and set out for California. They hoped for work harvesting crops in the vast fruit and vegetable farms of that state's Imperial Valley or picking cotton in the Central Valley.

It was a difficult and dangerous journey. In the words of one historian, "The smallest mishap—a blown tire, a cracked carburetor, a child's illness—could take every penny and leave [a family] stranded and friendless."

Many of those who made it to California faced hardship and sometimes hostility from local people. Those who found work were often paid as little as forty cents for picking a hundred pounds of cotton. Often the entire family, including the youngest children, had to work to earn enough to buy food to see them through to the next day of backbreaking labor.

The plight of the "Okies" (so-called because many came from Oklahoma) attracted national attention. This was partly due to the work of photographers employed by such New Deal agencies as the Farm Security Administration (FSA). Their faces can still be seen in the work of Dorothea Lange and Arthur Rothstein. Through their lenses they captured unforgettable images of the life on the road, in the fields, and in the crowded and often unsanitary migrant camps. The migration from the Dust Bowl also inspired John Steinbeck's great novel *The Grapes of Wrath*, which was later made into a powerful movie.

For many Americans, the Great Depression strengthened family ties. Living on the edge of poverty, everyone—children included—contributed whatever they could to the family's finances. Older kids and teenagers delivered newspapers or groceries, babysat,

YEARS OF DUST

RESETTLEMENT ADMINISTRATION
Rescues Victims
Restores Land to Proper Use

Roosevelt launched the Resettlement Administration to help families hurt by dust storms. (Library of Congress)

or shoveled snow and mowed lawns for more prosperous neighbors. One historian estimates that in 1930s California, half of all teenage boys and a quarter of all teenage girls held some kind of part-time job. If both parents were working (or looking for work), older children cared for their younger brothers and sisters and did much of the housework.

With little money for leisure activities, families relied on themselves for entertainment, too. In the boom years of the 1920s, Dad might have spent his free time on the golf course. Mom might have shopped while the kids hung out at a soda fountain. A decade later, the same family might spend its leisure hours gathered around the radio (if they had managed to keep up the payments), playing checkers or board games, or just talking.

Having to depend on one another for survival brought a special sense of togetherness to many American families. Indeed, many people who grew up in the 1930s remember the Depression years as a time when shared hardship drew family members closer.

Chapter Two

Social and Political Attitudes

The 1920s were known as the "Roaring Twenties" because of the pace of change and the carefree attitude that many members of society seemed to hold. A magazine cover from 1928 (LEFT) shows a young woman in a short dress dancing with an older man. When the Great Depression began, ending the Roaring Twenties, many Americans looked to President Franklin Roosevelt (RIGHT) for inspiration. With his wife, Eleanor, urging him on, Roosevelt established many new programs to help Americans get back on their feet. (Library of Congress)

On April 15, 1920, armed robbers shot and killed two security guards outside the Slater & Morrill shoe factory in South Braintree, Massachusetts. The killers grabbed the $16,000, which was the payroll for the factory's workers. Then they stole a car and fled the scene.

Three weeks later, police arrested Nicola Sacco and Bartolomeo Vanzetti and charged them with the crime. In July 1920, the two were found guilty and sentenced to death. Over the next six years, Sacco and Vanzetti's lawyers repeatedly appealed the verdict and fought for a retrial. But even though new evidence had come to light, there would be no new trial. On August 23, 1927, Sacco and Vanzetti went to their deaths in the electric chair.

This was no ordinary robbery-and-murder case. Sacco and Vanzetti's long legal battle had captured the nation's attention. Their execution sparked protests not only in America but also around the world. To many people, Sacco and Vanzetti died not because of what they had done, but because of who they were.

First, they were immigrants—both had come to America from Italy in 1908. They were also political radicals. Sacco and Vanzetti were anarchists—they believed in the overthrow of the U.S. government and the nation's capitalist economic system.

Sacco and Vanzetti's supporters argued that the two had not been given a fair trial. They claimed that police and the prosecutors had concentrated more on the men's immigrant origins and political beliefs than on evidence linking them to the crime.

Fear of the Foreign

The controversy over Sacco and Vanzetti reflected deep divisions in American society in the 1920s and 1930s. It was an era when America turned inward, largely ignoring events in the world beyond its shores. This attitude is called isolationism. At the same time, within America itself, many people feared that "foreign" ideas and influences posed a danger to "the American way of life." This fear played a big part not only in the Sacco and Vanzetti case but also in many of the major social and political issues of the era.

These attitudes had their roots in America's involvement in World War I. The United States only entered the war in its last year and a half, and following much debate. Americans were urged to fight Germany "to make the world safe for democracy." After the war ended in November 1918, the world seemed neither safe nor democratic to many Americans.

Partly as a result of this feeling, the Senate rejected the treaty that ended the war. It would have committed the United States to membership in the League of Nations, an international peacekeeping organization. Americans would not return in force to the international scene until another world war began twenty years later.

The Red Scare

Americans were also troubled by another side effect of World War I: the Russian Revolution. In 1917, Russia's Communist Party, the Bolsheviks, seized power. The world's first communist state, the Soviet Union, came into being. The Bolsheviks promised to support similar movements in countries like the United States. Americans now worried that immigrant "Reds" planned to start a revolution. (Red was the color of international communism.)

To some Americans, communism, socialism, and anarchism seemed much the same thing. The fact that many socialists and anarchists were immigrants from Eastern and Southern Europe fueled fears of foreign "agitators" operating here. This fear was not totally groundless. A series of violent attacks took place across America in 1919 and 1920.

The federal government responded by arresting thousands of suspected "radicals" across the country in the so-called "Palmer raids," named for Attorney General A. Mitchell Palmer. The raids peaked on January 1, 1920, when about 4,000 people were rounded up. Many were jailed without being charged. This was in violation of their constitutional rights. Those of foreign birth were deported (forced to leave the country). When the revolution didn't happen, fear lost its grip on the American public. The "Red Scare" ended. Most of those jailed were freed by President Warren Harding after he took office in 1921.

Closing the Door

Fear of "foreign" ideas and influences also led to an end to the massive immigration to the United States between the end of the Civil War and the beginning of World War I. Despite the fact that everyone except Native Americans was descended from people who had come from somewhere else, many people of "old American stock" felt that the recent newcomers would never be "real" Americans.

The earlier Americans were of mainly British or other northern European ancestry. The new Americans came from places like Poland and Russia and Italy. The old Americans were largely Protestant Christian. The new Americans were mostly Roman Catholic, Eastern Orthodox, or Jewish. The old Americans tended to live on farms and in small towns and to make their living from the land. The new Americans crowded into cities and worked in factories and shops.

The old Americans spoke English. Many new Americans continued to use the language of their homelands. The newcomers also brought with them some customs and traditions that the old Americans found strange and "un-American." In many communities there was deep prejudice against immigrants.

When World War I ended and immigrants again began arriving, a movement to restrict immigration gathered strength. In 1921, Congress passed the "Quota Act." The idea behind this law was to "freeze" the ethnic makeup of the country as it was before the war. Immigration from each nation was now limited to no more than 3 percent of the total number of people from that nation living in the United States in 1910.

"I lift my lamp beside the golden door," reads the poem engraved at the base of the Statue of Liberty in New York Harbor—the first sight of America for millions of immigrants. Congress now began closing the door. In 1924, the Johnson-Reed Act closed it further by cutting each nation's quota to 2 percent. In 1929, a "national origins" law all but slammed the door shut by limiting immigration to no more than 150,000 people per year from the entire world.

Immigration wasn't much of an issue in the 1930s. The depression-ravaged United States offered little opportunity to newcomers. In fact, during the 1930s, more people left the country than arrived as immigrants.

For one group of people, however, the chance to come to America could mean the difference between life and death. These were Jews and members of other groups fleeing Nazi Germany and German-occupied parts of Europe. A number of famous

In this cartoon, Uncle Sam guards entrance to the United States from Europe. Under the Immigration Act of 1924, the number of immigrants from any one Southern or Eastern European country could only equal 3 percent of the population of immigrants from that country already in the United States. Immigration from Asia was banned almost completely. (Library of Congress)

refugees did reach safety and freedom here in the 1930s. They included scientists Albert Einstein and Enrico Fermi, movie director Billy Wilder, writer Thomas Mann, and orchestra conductor Arturo Toscanini.

These immigrants and many others greatly enriched America's cultural and scientific life. But they were the lucky few. Even when reports of large-scale killing of European Jews reached America, Congress didn't change the quotas to allow more immigration of people at risk. A 1939 bill to admit 20,000 Jewish children never came to a vote in Congress. And in 1940, the ocean liner *St. Louis*, with 900 refugees aboard, was turned away in New York Harbor. Many of its passengers later died in the Holocaust.

Prohibition: Noble Experiment?

Fear of immigration and "foreign influences" also played a big part in one of the biggest issues of the 1920s and 1930s—Prohibition. This was a national ban on making and selling alcoholic beverages.

Movements to limit or ban alcohol drinking were a part of the American scene from the early nineteenth century onward. The United States was a hard-drinking country in its early years, and many people were concerned about the effects of alcohol abuse. Supporters of Prohibition focused their anger on the saloons found in immigrant neighborhoods in the big cities and towns. To the Prohibitionists, the saloons were "dens of darkness and sin." By the time the United States entered World War I in 1917, seventeen states and many local governments had outlawed or strictly controlled the sale of alcohol. But this wasn't enough for the most passionate supporters of Prohibition. They wanted a national ban.

National prohibition would probably never have happened if not for World War I. Prohibition suddenly became a "patriotic" issue. Grain that might have gone into making beer and whiskey was now needed to feed American soldiers and European refugees. Also, many of the country's biggest beer brewers were of German ancestry.

In December 1917, Congress passed the Eighteenth Amendment to the Constitution. It outlawed the "sale, manufacture, and transport of intoxicating liquors." The amendment was

**Federal agents
destroy an illegal
supply of alcohol
during Prohibition.**
(Library of Congress)

ratified about a year later. Another federal law, the Volstead Act, defined an "intoxicating liquor" as any beverage with more than 1 percent alcohol. This included beer and wine as well as whiskey and other spirits.

Historians debate just how well Prohibition worked, or whether it worked at all. There was certainly a huge drop in the amount of alcohol consumed during the thirteen years of Prohibition. The rate of certain types of crime fell too. So did the rate of alcohol-related mental and physical problems. But these gains hardly seem worth Prohibition's costs to American society.

The chief problem with Prohibition was that it was hard to enforce. Some people were going to drink regardless of the law. Many people began to make alcohol at home—so-called "bathtub gin." But most bought their alcohol from "bootleggers." These were criminals who made illegal alcohol or smuggled it in from Canada or Mexico or from ships off-coast.

It wasn't long before gangs of criminals realized that they could make huge profits by supplying drinkers with alcohol. Prohibition didn't create "organized crime" in America, but it made it into a big business. By the mid-1920s, heavily armed, well-organized gangs made and sold alcohol in all the major cities and many smaller communities. The gangs competed for customers and territories and settled their differences with guns and

Gangsters like Al Capone (LEFT) made fortunes from illegal alcohol during Prohibition. That was one of many reasons that people, including the young woman pictured (RIGHT), looked forward to Prohibition's end.
(Library of Congress)

bombs. Sometimes innocent people got caught in the crossfire.

Many of the gangs were made up of criminals from immigrant groups. For example, Irish, Italian, and Jewish gangs controlled most of the bootlegging in New York City and Chicago. Banning alcohol was supposed to make immigrant communities more "American." Instead, Prohibition wound up spreading violence and disrespect for the law into many American communities, immigrant and native-born alike.

Chicago was the most notorious city for gang violence. It had both a corrupt mayor (William "Big Bill" Thompson) and an especially brutal gang leader (Al Capone). Gang violence claimed up to 400 lives each year in Chicago during the late 1920s. Most of the casualties were members of gangs that had the poor judgment to compete with Capone's bootlegging operations. In the worst episode, the "St. Valentine's Day Massacre" of 1929, Capone's men gunned down seven members of a rival gang in a South Side garage.

The authorities could do little to make people respect the Prohibition law. The Bureau of the Internal Revenue, part of the Treasury Department, had the unhappy job of enforcing Prohibition. But there were too few agents, too little money, too much territory to cover, and too many people willing to break the law to buy a drink or sell one. In addition, Prohibition agents were paid little, so many found it hard to turn down a bribe. Bootleggers also bribed or threatened local judges and police officers into "looking the other way."

"Speakeasies"—illegal drinking clubs—sprang up everywhere. Massachusetts, for example, had about 1,000 saloons before Prohibition. By 1930 there may have been as many as 8,000 speakeasies in the state—4,000 in Boston alone.

Illegal drinking was not just a problem in the cities. "Even in the most remote country districts," journalist H. L. Mencken wrote in 1924, "there is absolutely no place in which any man who desires to drink alcohol cannot get it."

By the end of the 1920s, many people, including politicians in both major parties, considered Prohibition a failure. The "Noble Experiment," as it was called, seemed to be doing more harm than good. But supporters of Prohibition still formed an influential group. Even politicians who had private doubts about Prohibition felt they had to support it publicly. In 1930, Congress conducted a study of Prohibition, but the results were confusing. The official report seemed to say that while Prohibition wasn't working, it should be continued anyway.

In the end, the Great Depression killed Prohibition. The economic slump led to a sharp drop in the amount of taxes collected in many communities. Politicians realized that relegalizing alcohol and taxing sales would help make up the shortfall. An amendment to overturn the Eighteenth Amendment passed Congress and went to the states for ratification. The Twenty-First Amendment became law in December 1933. America's dry spell had finally ended.

Ku Klux Klan and "100 percent Americanism"

Anti-immigrant feeling in the 1920s did not just find expression in immigration restriction and Prohibition. It also surfaced in white robes and hoods in the form of the "revived" Ku Klux Klan.

The original Ku Klux Klan was founded after the Civil War by former Confederate officers to keep the newly freed slaves "in their place" through violence and terror. After World War I, the new Klan borrowed old costumes and rituals as well as hatred of African Americans. It added new targets: immigrants, Jews, Catholics, and anybody else who wasn't native-born, white, Protestant, and "100 percent American" by Klan standards.

For a few years, the new Klan enjoyed widespread popularity. By 1924, it claimed a membership of more than 4 million. Most lived in the South and Midwest, but there were groups through-

Female members of the Ku Klux Klan march in Washington, D.C. While the original Civil War–era Klan had focused on attacks on African Americans, by the 1920s, Klan members also preached hatred of Jews, Catholics, Asians, and all other non-Protestant immigrants to the United States. (Library of Congress)

out the country.

The Klan kept up its traditions of cross burnings, beatings, and lynchings, but it also went into politics. In many communities, winning an election was impossible without Klan support. By the mid-1920s, Klan influence reached into the legislatures and governors' mansions of several states.

The Klan's power faded fast after 1925, when its "Grand Dragon" leader was convicted of a brutal murder. Many Klan members had already realized that the organization's leaders were more interested in making money than in "100 percent Americanism." By the end of the decade, Klan membership was down to a handful of diehard racists.

Hard Times, Extreme Politics

Concern over radicalism faded amid the prosperity of the 1920s. But it returned during the Great Depression. In the fearful years of the 1930s, some people came to believe that only extreme political, social, and economic measures would ease hunger, homelessness, and unemployment. They argued that the stock-market crash and the economic collapse that followed proved that capitalism and democracy "didn't work."

Some pointed to Soviet-style communism as the way to go. By the end of the 1930s, the Communist Party of the USA (CPUSA) claimed a membership of 100,000. Even Americans who did not belong to the CPUSA felt that communists had to be doing something right. The Soviet Union seemed to have full employment at a time when millions of Americans were jobless. The humorist Will Rogers summed up this feeling: "Those rascals in Russia... have got some mighty good ideas. Imagine a whole country going to work!"

The communists and their supporters ignored reports that under its ruthless dictator, Joseph Stalin, the Soviet Union was basically a huge prison. Millions of people were starved to death, shot, or sent to concentration camps. When the Soviet Union became an ally of Nazi Germany in September 1939, the CPUSA's influence in America was all but destroyed.

After 1933, Germany seemed to some to have beaten its own economic depression through the "National Socialist" (Nazi) program of Adolf Hitler. But by the mid-1930s, Nazi Germany was moving toward war with its neighbors and preparing for the mass murder of millions of Jews and other peoples.

The Soviet Union's dictator, Joseph Stalin, killed millions of his own citizens during his long rule. (Library of Congress)

This did not prevent a very small number of Americans of German birth or ancestry from joining pro-Nazi organizations like the German-American Bund. The Bund was run from Germany's capital, Berlin, in the same way that the CPUSA was run from Moscow, the capital of the Soviet Union.

There was plenty of homegrown radicalism to go around in the 1930s. "Rabble-rousers" (people trying to rouse the anger of the American public), of all kinds were part of the American scene throughout the decade.

There was Father Charles Coughlin, for example. Known as the "radio priest" for his fiery broadcasts from his Michigan church, Coughlin slammed "Franklin double-crossing Roosevelt" and promoted his own version of the New Deal, the National Union for Social Justice. His influence declined after he began blaming "Jewish bankers" for the country's economic problems.

Dr. Charles Townsend of California also won a national following for a time. Townsend's quick-fix solution for the Depression was for the federal government to give every retired American over the age of sixty $200 a month, which would be worth about $2,500 in 2003 money. The catch was that those who got the money would have to spend it all within thirty days. This scheme, Townsend argued, would both make life better for the nation's elderly and create jobs by boosting the economy.

Perhaps the most famous rabble-rouser of the 1930s was

Huey Long, a former governor of Louisiana. Long won election to the Senate in 1932. His program, "Share Our Wealth," called for the federal government to guarantee all Americans an income and provide free education, medical care, and other benefits. These were to be paid for by heavy taxes on "fortune holders." By the middle of the decade, there were 27,000 Share Our Wealth Clubs across the country. Long talked about running for president in 1936, but in September 1935 he was killed by an assassin.

President Roosevelt was reelected in 1936 by a landslide and again in 1940 by a smaller but still comfortable margin.

New Criminals, New Cops

The FBI "wanted" poster for John Dillinger, one of the most feared criminals in American history.
(Library of Congress)

Gang violence fell after Prohibition ended in 1933, but it didn't disappear. In many cities, bootlegging gangs applied the violent skills they had developed to new areas of crime—drugs, gambling, and prostitution.

In the desperate depression years, a new kind of criminal caught the public's attention. This was the "motorized gang" who roamed the back roads of the Midwest and Southwest, driving powerful cars and robbing banks by gunpoint.

Motorized gang bandits included Bonnie Parker and Clyde Barrow, John Dillinger, George "Baby Face" Nelson, and Arthur "Pretty Boy" Floyd. To some Americans, they were modern Robin Hoods who stole from the rich and gave to the poor. In fact, they robbed from everybody and gunned down anyone who got in their way.

Because these mobile criminals often crossed state lines, the federal government got involved. The Federal Bureau of Investigation (FBI) was established in 1924, with J. Edgar Hoover as its director. Hoover and his G-men (for "government") won fame in 1934, when FBI agents shot gangster John Dillinger outside a Chicago movie theater.

Toward a National Culture

Although American society was deeply divided in many ways, it began to develop a truly national culture. New technologies, forms of communication, and business practices helped break down the old regional differences in the country. In all parts of the nation, North and South, East and West, people were familiar with the same movies, listened to the same radio programs, and shopped in the same chain stores. Where people lived still played a big part in how they lived. But by the end of the 1930s, Americans had more in common than ever before.

Travel played a big part in this development. In the 1920s, affordable cars, improved roads, and more leisure time for working Americans led to a huge boom in travel and tourism. Air travel went from being a novelty to an established form of transportation. By 1929, Americans could get from coast to coast, using a combination of trains and planes, in a then-amazing three days.

Meanwhile, radio brought the country into America's living rooms. The first commercial radio station, Pittsburgh's KDKA, began broadcasting in 1920. By 1926, the first nationwide network, the National Broadcasting Company (NBC), was on the air. Three more national networks had joined NBC by 1939.

Before the 1920s, few businesses operated nationwide. The food people ate, the clothes they wore, and the furnishings in their homes were usually local products. In the 1920s, "chain" stores revolutionized the way Americans shopped. The same products were now available almost everywhere, in greater variety and often at lower cost than in old-style stores. Woolworths, A&P, Piggly Wiggly, Safeway, and J.C. Penney were either founded or expanded greatly during these years.

Even more important, movies contributed to the making of a natural culture. Americans were movie-mad in the 1920s. About 50 million people (close to half the population) went to the movies at least once a week. That number dropped only slightly during the Depression.

Americans in Seattle, New Orleans, Des Moines, and everywhere in between—immigrant and native-born alike—laughed at Charlie Chaplin and cheered cowboy star Tom Mix. They all listened as Al Jolson, star of *The Jazz Singer*, the first "talkie" movie, proclaimed, "You ain't heard nothin' yet!"

In the end, movies united Americans more than Prohibition or any political or social movement. They brought immigrants and their children into the mainstream of American society and united the farmer and the city dweller. Along with radio, Model Ts, and mass marketing, they laid the foundations of the American popular culture that continues to flourish in the twenty-first century.

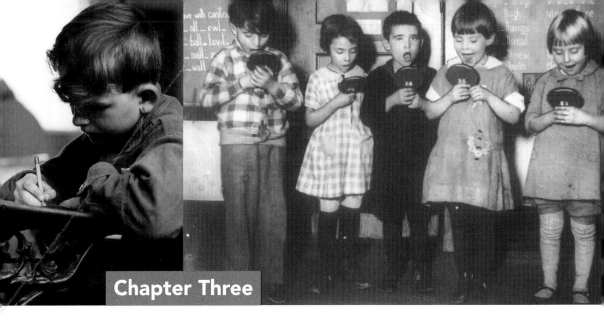

Chapter Three

Education

The 1920s were boom times for American schools as well as for the economy. There was great growth in American education from elementary schools to universities.

Between 1920 and 1930, school attendance from kindergarten through high school rose by more than 5 million, from about 23 million to about 28 million. More children and young adults went to school than ever before in the nation's history. On average, they stayed in school longer while learning a wider variety of subjects.

The State of Education in 1920

The education boom of the 1920s was the result of events that had begun many decades earlier. The idea that all children should be able, or even required, to attend school took a long time to gain acceptance everywhere in America.

By the middle of the nineteenth century, however, most states had passed school attendance laws. Parents were required to enroll children in schools for at least a few years of basic education. But it wasn't until the decades after the Civil War that free public education became available to most American children. (Public schools are supported by taxes and open to all the children of a particular community. In the 1920s and 1930s, about 90 percent of all U.S. children in school attended public schools.)

Even then, up until the 1920s, many American children left

school at very early ages to go to work to help their families make ends meet. In the early 1900s, however, many states and eventually the federal government passed laws restricting child labor. The combination of school attendance laws and child-labor laws put more children in school. In 1925, the U.S. Supreme Court made school attendance mandatory (required) for all American children up to age sixteen. By then, more than 85 percent of children ages five through seventeen went to school.

Changes in Teaching

Teaching, too, changed greatly in the decades before the 1920s. In the 1800s, most teachers were male. Over time, female teachers with a high school education became the norm. They were willing to work for less money than men, and they were thought to provide children with better role models for life. After the Civil War, many states founded teacher's colleges or "normal schools" to prepare teachers. By 1915, all the states required special training for teachers, and growing numbers of teachers had four-year college degrees.

At the same time, groups like the National Educational Association worked to introduce "scientific" methods of teaching and to raise teaching to the status of a profession similar to medicine and law. As a result, average salaries for teachers rose from about $800 per year in 1920 to almost $1,500 in 1940. Nevertheless, teachers' pay remained lower than other professions.

The ways teachers taught also changed during the 1920s and 1930s. Rote learning had long been the most common teaching method. Students were instructed to memorize and recite information, such as the multiplication tables or the capitals of the states. But by the 1920s, institutions like Columbia University's Teachers College in New York City had begun to spread more "progressive" theories of education to many schools around the country.

The new teaching methods focused on problem-solving skills. Students were taught how to "learn by doing," rather than just memorize information. However, rote learning remained the rule in many classrooms, especially in the early grades.

Rural Schools

Before the 1920s, educating rural children posed many problems. On most farms, the entire family shared the work of

Students pose with their teacher, Mrs. Lenore Waltermire, in Wheat Ridge, Jefferson County, Colorado, in about 1915. (Library of Congress)

tending crops and caring for animals. Children might be able to go to school for only a few months of the year—usually the winter months, between harvesting and planting.

With rural households spread out over a wide area, schoolchildren often had to walk a mile or more to get to school. Rural schools typically didn't have separate grades for children of different ages and separate classes for different subjects. Instead students of all ages crowded into one room in which a single teacher taught all subjects.

The arrival of the automobile age transformed rural education, just as it did so many aspects of daily life. For schoolchildren in the countryside, it was not the car but the tractor and the school bus that led to the greatest changes in education.

By 1930, there were almost a million tractors in use on America's farms. Tractors and other machinery made farm families less dependent on their own labor. This allowed children more time for schooling.

Even more important was the school bus. The bus allowed many children from a wide area to attend one big school. In these "consolidated" schools, students could be taught by age group, and they were staffed by teachers who specialized in different subjects.

The school bus narrowed the "education gap" between rural areas and towns and cities. It made the old one-room rural schoolhouse a thing of the past. At the start of the 1920s, there were about 200,000 one-room, one-teacher schools in America. That number had fallen to less than 100,000 by 1940.

Primary Education, 1920–1940

American public education has always been run at a local level. The structure of school systems often differed from community to community in the 1920s and 1930s, as it does today. But in general, public school systems were divided into primary schools (usually called elementary schools) and secondary schools (high schools). This period also saw the spread of junior high schools. They had begun around 1910 as a kind of "bridge" between elementary school and high school.

For many children, education began when they entered kindergarten, usually at the age of five. The idea for kindergarten was imported from Germany in the 1870s. (The term means "children's garden" in German.) The first public kindergartens served mainly the children of immigrants in poor neighborhoods in big cities. By the 1920s, kindergarten was a regular part of the school system in many American communities. During that decade, the number of children in kindergarten rose from 481,000 to 723,000.

After kindergarten, a child began the first of six grades of elementary school. The typical elementary school curriculum (course of studies) included traditional subjects like English, history, math, and science. In the 1920s, many school curricula included new subjects, especially civics—the study of the American system of government.

This change was due in part to the writings of philosopher John Dewey. In books like *Democracy and Education* (1916), Dewey argued that American schools should do more than just teach the basic "academic" subjects. Dewey believed schools should also teach young people how to be good citizens, ready to meet the challenges of life in American society.

Before automobiles were common, travel to school was much more difficult for young people living in the countryside. By the late 1920s, schoolbuses had become more common. They allowed children, like these students from King City Union High School in Salinas Valley, California, to travel great distances to get to a central school. Their bus stopped at a gas station to pick up about twelve students. Many of them were driven to the bus stop by their parents. (Library of Congress)

Americanizing through Education

John Dewey
(Library of Congress)

The idea that public schools had a mission to produce "good Americans" took on special meaning in communities with large immigrant populations. Federal laws practically halted immigration in the 1920s (see Chapter 2). There were still many children who had been born overseas or to immigrant parents. This was a time in which many native-born Americans believed the nation should be a "melting pot" in which people from many different nations and cultures would take on a common "American" identity.

Schools sought to "Americanize" their students by promoting patriotism. In many schools, the day began with the pledge of allegiance. (In 1924, the first part of the pledge was changed from "I pledge allegiance to the flag" to "I pledge allegiance to the flag of the United States of America.") Often the pledge was followed by a reading from the Bible or a prayer.

History textbooks of the era stressed America's "special" role in the world. They celebrated the heroic doings of figures like George Washington and Abraham Lincoln. Classroom activities often centered on American traditions and holidays. For example, the writer Alfred Kazin, the son of Russian Jewish parents who had emigrated to Brooklyn, recalled his school days in the 1920s: "Thanksgiving was unknown at home, it was hardly one of the Jewish holidays. Nevertheless at school Thanksgiving was something terrific. We would cut out little figures of the Pilgrims . . . and put these on the windows of the school. On the other hand, it would never have occurred to us to bring our [Jewish] holidays into the schoolroom . . . . "

Public schools also tried to Americanize immigrant children by teaching all classes in the English language. Before the 1920s, schools in communities with big immigrant populations often conducted classes in the language of the community's largest immigrant group as well as in English. In 1917, however, New York City's public school system—in which almost three-quarters of the students were children of immigrants—adopted an "English only" policy.

The Changing American High School

Although the number of high-school graduates in America tripled between 1900 and 1920, only about one in five Americans had high-school degrees in 1920. (About one in four had college degrees in the year 2000.) It was not until 1929 that a majority of high-school-aged Americans actually attended high school. Even then, less than a third actually graduated.

Before the 1920s, the chief role of most American high schools was to prepare students for college. Because only a small number of students went on to college, high-school enrollment levels were low. Most high schools concentrated on teaching "academic" subjects that were thought to give students the background to succeed in college.

In the 1920s and 1930s, however, the role of the high school in American education changed. Instead of just preparing a few students for college, high schools also became places where many young people prepared for a life in the workplace.

One of the forces behind this change was the National Education Association's 1918 report on secondary education. The report argued that in addition to teaching "fundamental processes" like reading and writing, American high schools should also instruct students in health, family life, vocation (technical training for specific jobs), citizenship, "ethical character" (good behavior), and "worthy use of leisure time."

As a result, subjects like literature and foreign languages became less important in high school curricula during the 1920s and 1930s. There was a new emphasis on technical and work-related subjects. It was still generally accepted that some jobs (woodworking, metalworking, and other "mechanical arts") were for boys, and others (typing, "home economics," cooking, sewing, and other household skills) were for girls. However, by the late 1920s, some schools had begun to teach girls skills like auto mechanics, traditionally thought of as masculine.

Hygiene Class

The movement to Americanize immigrant children in the schools went beyond promoting patriotism and the English language. In an era before antibiotics, and in cities where many poorer families had to share washing, cooking, and toilet facilities, diseases claimed many children's lives. The need to fight disease led many city schools to take an interest in students' physical health. Classes in "hygiene" stressed the importance of keeping clean and avoiding germs. Washing hands before lunch and brushing teeth afterward became a school day ritual. One woman who went to public schools in the New York City borough of the Bronx in the 1930s remembers lining up with her classmates every morning so the teacher could inspect their fingernails for dirt.

Poster promoting good oral hygiene, from about 1936. (Library of Congress)

In the early twentieth century, schools began to teach practical skills in addition to subjects like English, math, and science. At Central High School in Washington, D.C., in 1927, Grace Hurd, Evelyn Harrison, and Corinna DiJiulian (LEFT TO RIGHT) and Grace Wagner (UNDER CAR) learned the art of auto mechanics. (Library of Congress)

Tracking and Testing

Most high schools began to divide their student bodies into two groups. One group was expected to go on to college. Those pupils studied the "academic" subjects. The other group was expected to enter the workforce after leaving school. They took "vocational," or work-related, subjects. This system became known as "tracking."

How would school administrators decide which "track" a particular student should take? The new science of intelligence testing seemed to offer a way. Intelligence testing on a large scale first took place during World War I, when the U.S. Army gave soldiers "I.Q." tests to measure their mental fitness for different military jobs. (The term *I.Q.* stood for Intelligence Quotient.) The higher a person's I.Q., the better equipped that person was to master complex subjects—or so it was thought at the time.

By the 1920s, many public school systems were using I.Q. tests to determine the "track" each student would follow. The tests were usually given in the primary grades, but their results determined a student's educational future for as long as he or she stayed in school. Those who scored well on I.Q. tests were "tracked" for college when they reached high school. Those with lower scores went on the vocational track.

Aside from the flaws of the testing-and-tracking system,

the big changes in high school education in the 1920s and 1930s had many positive results. Before the 1920s, as previously discussed, relatively few American children attended school beyond the primary grades. There was a huge rise in high school enrollment and graduation rates between World War I and World War II. For the first time, millions of young Americans received an education beyond basic "reading, writing, and arithmetic."

The new high schools also gave young people more than practical work skills. They introduced their students to art and music and gave them the opportunity to participate in organized sports, theater groups, and other extracurricular (outside of classes) activities.

Higher Education: Colleges and Universities

Although the number of college students rose from about 600,000 in 1920 to 1.5 million in 1940, relatively few young Americans saw the inside of a college classroom during these decades. Only about one in five high-school graduates went on to college in the 1920s. That percentage dropped as the Great Depression set in.

Young Americans who did go to college were mainly from prosperous middle- and upper-class families. But more Americans than ever were in college, so life on the college campus began to work its way into America's popular imagination.

Extracurricular activities like school sports were introduced to more schools in the 1920s. A junior high school girls basketball team (LEFT) **poses in 1926. Columbia University's football team brushes up on tackling during an early season practice in the 1930s.** (Library of Congress)

In the popular view, the typical "college man" of the 1920s was more likely to be found cheering on his school's football team or dancing with a co-ed (female student) at a fraternity party than studying. College fashions like raccoon-skin coats and baggy pants spread well beyond the campus. Movies, "college humor" magazines, and the popular drawings of John Held, Jr., all depicted college students as more interested in a good time than a good education.

There was some truth in this image. In the boom years, many college students looked on college as a kind of four-year vacation. Many professors saw little point in challenging their students. Reporter Vincent Sheean later wrote of his years at the University of Chicago: "Within those [walls] what, after all, had I learned? . . . Not much. I had some vague idea of history and philosophy, a bowing acquaintance with English and French literature . . . . I had acquired half a dozen friends—perhaps. I had learned how to dance the fox trot."

Only a small percentage of college students attended elite institutions. Apart from a few students on scholarships, only young people from the wealthiest families could afford the cost of tuition. Many top schools at this time limited admission in other ways. For example, some universities, including Harvard, restricted the number of Jewish students to a small percentage of the student body.

The majority of American college students in the 1920s and 1930s went to smaller private colleges operated by religious denominations. Some students attended public state colleges and universities. These state schools were sometimes called land grant colleges, after an 1862 act of Congress that gave individual states federal lands to sell to raise funds for higher education. At these schools, tuition was less expensive.

Students arrive at Dunbarton College, a Catholic women's college, in about 1920. (Library of Congress)

Many cities made higher

education available to their residents. New York's City College system, probably the finest system of its kind, offered free tuition and open admissions. It gave students from the city's many immigrant families a great opportunity to get ahead in the world.

Just as public high schools of the time broadened their curricula to include vocational subjects, these public colleges and universities prepared graduates to be teachers, farmers, engineers, scientists, nurses, and businesspeople. Private schools tended to focus on traditional liberal arts degrees.

Even during the boom years, many students at the smaller private colleges and at state schools found it hard to meet the cost of tuition, books, and room and board. Students at these institutions were more likely to spend their time outside the classroom working to earn money rather than going to football games and parties.

African American Education

Most African Americans lived in the South during the 1920s and 1930s, and southern states spent less on education than states in other parts of the country. Spending on education for African American children was especially low. One historian estimates that some Southern counties spent $1 for African American education for every $40 spent on education for white children during the 1920s.

This was a reflection of the racist attitudes of many white southern politicians. Mississippi governor Theodore Bilbo, meanly said that too much education "spoils a good field hand." By this he meant that if African Americans had access to education, they would come to want more out of life than backbreaking work in the cotton fields.

As a result of these attitudes, fewer African American children attended school than white children. Southern school systems were also segregated. This meant that African American and white students attended separate schools.

In an 1894 case, the U.S. Supreme Court declared that segregation was legal as long as accommodations for both races were "separate but equal." In fact, southern schools were always separate but rarely equal. The quality of education for African American children was almost always lower than for whites. Conditions in African American schools did begin to improve in some places during the mid-1930s as a result of the New Deal.

Education for African Americans was not unequal only in the South. The children of African Americans who had moved north in the Great Migration faced many of the same unequal conditions as the children of those who had remained in the South.

Opportunities for African Americans in higher education were also limited. Many colleges and universities admitted only small numbers of African American students, so most such students attended institutions like the Tuskegee Institute in Alabama, Howard University in Washington, D.C., and Fisk University in Nashville, Tennessee, which had been founded for African Americans.

There was a small victory for African American access in higher education in 1938, when the Supreme Court ruled that the University of Missouri had to establish a law school for African American students if it had one for its white students. However, it would not be until 1954 that the Supreme Court ruled that segregation was illegal in public education at all levels.

Education in the Depression

The Great Depression hit American education hard. As the number of unemployed people rose in the early 1930s, taxes collected by local governments fell. Because public schools are supported by taxes, this meant that some communities could not pay their teachers or even keep their schools open.

In New York City, 300,000 children were sent home in 1932 because the public school system ran out of money. The city of Chicago could only pay its teachers with bonds—pieces of paper that promised that they'd be paid in cash when times got better. Across the country, perhaps as many as 200,000 teachers lost their jobs in the early 1930s.

The number of young Americans graduating from high school went up during the Depression. Before the hard times began, many high school students left school at sixteen or seventeen to go to work. But with few jobs available, more students stayed on until graduation. By 1940, for the first time in American history, half of eighteen-year-old Americans had a high school degree.

Fewer of these graduates were going on to college, though.

The number of college students fell as the number of jobless people rose. Parents who now had to worry about making ends meet were unable to pay for higher education. In addition, the high unemployment rate meant that a college degree no longer guaranteed a graduate a good job—or any job at all.

This was especially true for young women. The percentage of women attending college rose steadily in the decades from about 1870 to 1920. (In fact, in 1920, almost half of America's college students were women.) But after 1929, the number of women in college dropped dramatically. Despite the growing numbers of women in the workforce, most jobs were still open mostly to men. Many parents who would have sent their daughters to college earlier now saw no reason to do so: If so many male college graduates couldn't get jobs, what chance did a woman graduate have?

Many students, male and female, who stayed in college struggled to pay tuition. By the early 1930s, the carefree years of the 1920s were just a memory on most campuses.

Pauline Kael, later a famous writer about the movies, remembered what it was like at the University of California at Berkeley in the 1930s: "There were kids who didn't have a place to sleep, huddled under bridges on the campus. I had a scholarship, but there were times when I didn't have any food. . . . I remember feeding other kids by cooking up more spaghetti than I can ever consider again."

During the 1930s, some university professors came to Washington, D.C., to help President Franklin Roosevelt establish the New Deal. Earlier presidents had sometimes turned to the nation's universities for advice, but FDR was the first president to recruit a large number of professors into his administration.

The president's "Brain Trust" included Rexford Tugwell of Columbia University. Tugwell became head of the Resettlement Administration, which helped farmers who had lost their land. Another was David Lilienthal of Harvard, who became one of the directors of the Tennessee Valley Authority (TVA). This new relationship between the federal government and higher education was yet another way in which the New Deal changed American society.

Chapter Four

The Economy

A long period of prosperity ended in 1929 when the stock market crashed, sending New York's Wall Street (LEFT) and then the rest of the country into a panic. During the late 1930s, when this billboard (RIGHT) appeared, the nation had been through a decade of economic depression, making its optimistic message appear out of place. (Library of Congress)

The "boom and bust" the American people experienced in the 1920s and 1930s is above all a story of economics. In the 1920s, thriving industries and an ever-rising stock market created a period of prosperity some Americans thought would last forever. Then, in a very short time, most of the gains of the boom years were wiped out.

Car sales drove the American economy in the 1920s. More than anything else, the automobile powered the boom that lasted from about 1921 to 1929. Thanks to improved production methods (largely developed by Henry Ford), cars could be made quickly, in huge numbers, and at prices working people could afford (see Chapter 2). By 1929, 26.5 million cars rolled along America's roads and streets. Five out of six cars in the world were American made. All the industries involved in making cars and keeping them going—oil, rubber, steel, and other metals—shared in this amazing growth.

The radio industry was another big economic success story of the 1920s. In 1920, when the first regular radio broadcasts began, Americans spent about $10 million on radios. Spending on radios rose to almost $500 million by the end of the decade.

With sales of cars, radios, and other goods soaring, manufacturers were able to employ more workers and pay them better. In 1923, for example, the giant U.S. Steel Corporation hired 17,000 workers while also reducing their workday from twelve to eight hours and raising wages. Not all workers were so lucky, but average income (wages and other earnings) for Americans rose by about 25 percent between 1921 and 1929. More people had more money to spend than ever before, and American consumers had many more products to buy.

Life on the Installment Plan

The 1920s brought a new way to buy goods—the "pay as you go," or installment plan. Instead of having to pay for a car, an appliance, or a piece of furniture all at once, many stores and mail-order companies now let buyers make a small down payment and pay the rest off over time. This was usually in monthly installments. Americans no longer had to wait until they had saved enough money to make a major purchase. They could now enjoy a car, radio, or piano while they paid for it.

The growth of "pay as you go" purchasing made more goods available to more people, which helped to boost the economy. It also gave working-class Americans the chance to enjoy possessions that they couldn't otherwise have owned. But life on the installment plan had its drawbacks. The so-called "easy little payments" were often neither easy nor little. An installment purchase was a kind of loan. Just as banks charged interest on loans, stores charged buyers extra for the privilege of paying off a purchase over time. Buying an item on the installment plan, then, often meant paying more for it—sometimes as much as 50 percent more.

And, of course, buyers had to keep up the payments. During the boom years, when jobs were plentiful and wages were rising for most workers, many people thought they would have no problem in making payments. Later the Depression brought widespread unemployment. Installment payments often stretched family finances to the breaking point.

Even in the prosperous 1920s, many people gave in to the temptation to buy all things on the installment plan. This was done without considering just how much of their wages would have to go toward payments. For example, in a famous study of Muncie, Indiana, researchers found that many families were spending a quarter of their monthly income on car payments.

Critics charged that "pay as you go" plans encouraged Americans to live beyond their means. Earlier generations of

Americans had usually been wary about going into debt. But in the 1920s, the lure of "pay as you go" caused a big change in Americans' attitude toward debt. Between 1920 and 1929, the number of "time purchases" grew by an amazing 500 percent.

Businessmen and Boosters

Admiration for success in business was nothing new in American society, but it reached new heights in the 1920s. The decade was a kind of golden age for the American businessman.

By the time President Calvin Coolidge stated that "the chief business of America is business," many Americans enjoyed a rising standard of living. Politicians, the press, and much of the public showed their appreciation for this new prosperity by praising businesses and the men who ran them, from small-town merchants to the heads of major corporations.

Along with the admiration came support for the idea that businesses should be allowed to operate with little or no regulation from the government. In the Progressive Era, which lasted from about 1900 to 1917, many politicians and journalists had argued that the government needed to make sure that businesses operated in the public interest, not just to make profits.

Paul "Sunshine" Dietrick (ABOVE), was a popular speaker who traveled through America in the early 1920s, preaching the value of hard work, sacrifice, and commitment to business.
A Shriners Convention (BELOW) in 1920. Fraternal organizations became very popular in the 1920s.
(Library of Congress)

In the boom years, however, many people believed that it was in the best interests of society for government to take a "hands-off" attitude toward business. This philosophy is called laissez-faire, from the French for "leave it alone."

The growing admiration for business was also seen in the rise of "boosters" in communities across the country. These were businessmen and other community leaders who sought to promote

business growth in their towns and cities. "Boosters" joined together in organizations like the Shriners, the Rotary Club, Kiwanis, and Chambers of Commerce to urge citizens to support local businesses and attract new ones. These groups sponsored Boy and Girl Scout groups, raised money for local charities, and served as an important part of their members' social lives.

As long as the prosperity continued, however, most Americans continued to admire the nation's business leaders. As the economy grew year after year, it seemed to many people that American companies were helping to build a better society even as they made record-breaking profits. President Coolidge expressed this feeling in a 1925 speech to the New York City Chamber of Commerce. Business, said Coolidge, "rests squarely on the law of service. It has for its main reliance truth and faith and justice.... [It] is one of the greatest contributing forces to the moral and spiritual advancement of the [human] race."

Babbitt and Boosters

Not everyone admired "boosters," who worked to promote the values of local business. To some writers and critics, the average booster was dull, narrow-minded, and uninterested in the world beyond his office and the golf course. The title character of Sinclair Lewis' famous 1922 novel

Babbitt, a real-estate salesman in the fictional Midwestern city of Zenith, was just such a man.

Sinclair Lewis
(Library of Congress)

Artful Advertising

If business became almost a religion to some Americans in the 1920s, then advertising became almost an art form. Advertising—using media like newspapers and magazines to persuade consumers to buy goods and services—was well established before the 1920s. However, early advertisements were usually just product descriptions, written and illustrated in a fairly plain style.

Advertising became both more sophisticated and more widespread in the 1920s. Nationwide advertising agencies like Lord & Thomas, J. Walter Thompson, and Batten, Barton, Durstine & Osborn were formed. They began to use clever combinations of words, pictures, and psychology to convince consumers to buy their clients' products. By 1929, American companies were spending $3.5 billion a year on advertising.

The reason for this huge growth in advertising was simple. To keep sales growing, companies needed to convince Americans to spend their new wealth on consumer products. And because companies competed against each other for sales, each company tried to convince the consumer that its product—whether a car, an appliance, or a bar of soap—was better than the competitor's model.

Magazines like the *Saturday Evening Post, Better Homes and Gardens*, and *Ladies Home Journal* were especially important to the growth of advertising. Unlike local newspapers, these magazines were distributed across the country. This let advertisers reach a national audience. New printing methods allowed these magazines to print photographs and color artwork, which made advertisements more eye-catching.

If advertising was a near art form in the 1920s, then copywriters—who wrote the text—were advertising's poets. Instead of just listing a product's benefits, copywriters appealed to consumers' emotions.

A great example of this new kind of ad aimed to sell a new car called the Jordan Playboy. Appearing in the *Saturday Evening Post* in 1923, the ad's artwork was a simple drawing of a young woman in a car racing a cowboy on horseback. The ad's one hundred and seventy-three words began: "Somewhere west of Laramie, there's a bronco-busting, steer-roping girl who knows what I'm talking about." The remarkable thing about the ad was that it said almost nothing about the car itself. It did not tell the reader how many cylinders the car's engine had. It did not tell how many passengers the car could carry, or even how much it cost. Instead the ad tried to link a car in the reader's mind with a romantic view of the Wild West.

The new advertising also tried to create demand for products by playing on people's fears of being seen as unattractive or awkward. In 1914, for example, the Warner Lambert Company began selling a mouthwash called Listerine. Sales were slow until the early 1920s, when the company found that a medical publication had coined the term *halitosis* to describe bad breath. The company soon made halitosis a household word in a famous series of magazine ads. The ads made it seem as if bad breath doomed a sufferer to a life of loneliness. Listerine sales shot upward.

Although advertising had existed long before the 1920s, it had usually been limited to simple illustrations and longer descriptions of the products. The advertisement (TOP) for men's shirts places the man—and his shirt—in the rear. Instead the illustration focuses on his glamorous date. An advertisement (ABOVE) for ham featured art by the well-known illustrator Maxfield Parish. (Library of Congress)

Creating demand for products among new groups of consumers was another goal of 1920s advertisers. When many American women began to smoke cigarettes during the decade, tobacco companies quickly produced ads aimed at this new market. The makers of Lucky Strike cigarettes even promoted smoking as a way of losing weight with the slogan "Reach for a Lucky instead of a sweet!"

Advertisers also took advantage of new ways of communicating, especially radio, to sell products. In the first years of radio broadcasting, many people felt the airwaves should be "public property," free of advertising. In 1922, however, radio station WEAF in New York City began to sell "air time." On August 28 of that year, a local real-estate developer broadcast what was probably the first radio commercial.

As the number of radio listeners grew into the millions over the next few years, advertising invaded the airwaves. Sponsorship was the most common form of radio advertising in the 1920s and 1930s. A company would pay a radio station or network to have its name associated with a popular program or featured entertainer. In 1929, for example, listeners tuning into WEAF could hear Leopold Stokowski conduct the Philadelphia Symphony Orchestra, sponsored by the radio manufacturer Philco, or they could turn the dial to WJZ for a "musical melodrama" sponsored by Johnson & Johnson.

Chains across America

Like advertising, nationwide "chains" of stores weren't new in the 1920s. It was in this decade, however, that stores that sold the same goods at practically the same price everywhere became a familiar part of life for most consumers. These national businesses included gas stations (like Standard Oil, which had twelve stations in 1920 and 1,000 in 1929), department stores (like J.C. Penney's 312 stores in 1920, 1,395 in 1929), and stores that sold a variety of goods (like Woolworths 1,111 stores in 1920, 1,825 in 1929).

A gas station offers to fill automobile fuel tanks with Standard Oil. (Library of Congress)

Piggly Wiggly, a grocery chain, was the first to allow customers to choose their own purchases from shelves on the store floor. Beforehand, store employees had to retrieve whatever a customer wanted.
(Courtesy of Piggly Wiggly, Inc.)

The nation's improved road system helped the growth of the chains by making it easier to distribute goods nationwide. The chains also benefited from "economies of scale." Because they could purchase goods in huge quantities, the chains got better prices from producers than smaller, local stores. The chains could then pass on these savings to their customers in the form of lower prices.

Chain stores not only changed where most consumers shopped but also how they shopped. Before the 1920s, a customer in a grocery store usually had to ask a clerk for whatever he or she wanted to buy. The clerk would then bring the products from a shelf or storeroom. In the early 1920s, the grocery chain Piggly Wiggly (515 stores in 1920, 2,500 in 1929) introduced a new system it called "scientific merchandising." Piggly Wiggly did away with the clerks and put its shelves on the store floor, where the customer selected his or her own purchases. The self-service system saved time for the customer and reduced labor costs for Piggly Wiggly, because each store needed fewer employees. Within a few years, the rest of the chains adopted the new system. This marked the birth of the modern American supermarket.

Not everyone liked the chains. Owners of small local stores feared that the arrival of a chain store in their communities would drive them out of business. Community boosters in many towns urged citizens to "buy local." Most consumers, however, came to prefer the convenience, selection and, above all, the prices offered by chain stores.

ing. This hike in government spending did boost the economy, which grew every year from 1982 to 1990.

But Reagan combined high spending with deep tax cuts. As a result, the federal government spent more money than it took in every year. This forced the government to borrow money to pay for the added spending. The result was a huge deficit (the difference between income and spending.) By 1992, the government had to borrow nearly $300 billion. Some economists said this borrowing cut down on the amount of money businesses could borrow. As a result, they could not expand, which meant that they could not create more jobs. In addition, the government had to pay interest on its debt. By 1990, those payments totaled as much as $60 billion a year—money the government could not use to provide services. Many political leaders began to worry about these deficits. Finally, in 1987, Congress passed a law that required the government to balance the budget—making spending equal to receipts—by 1993.

In the early 1990s, another recession hit. This one lasted a little less than a year, but it came just as President George Bush was running for re-election. Voters felt that Bush did little to try to fix the slumping economy. Energetic Democrat Bill Clinton won the election in the fall of 1992. Clinton had good luck—he took office as the economy was already growing again. He also made good policy decisions, which helped that growth. He decided not to cut taxes and increased federal spending to create construction jobs across the country.

This stand helped gain the confidence of Alan Greenspan, the chairman of the Federal Reserve Board. The "Fed" is the nation's central bank. It sets rules that control interest rates and the money supply. Under Greenspan, the Fed cut interest rates. Business owners began to borrow and invest money to help their companies grow. One major investment was new technology. The personal computer had appeared in 1981. Soon, businesspeople began to use the new machines, finding new ways of doing work faster and more efficiently. Workers became more productive, able to finish more work in the same amount of time as before. This rise in productivity lowered the cost of doing business. Business profits rose. The economy began to grow at a faster rate. From 1992 until the end of the decade, the economy grew each year. Clinton took credit, calling it the longest period of sustained

Alan Greenspan
(Library of Congress)

growth in the country's history.

The economic boom brought more jobs to more people. During most of the 1980s, the unemployment rate—the percentage of people who wanted a job but could not find one—was 6 percent or higher. After a dip late in the decade, the rate spiked again in the early 1990s. It reached a high of 7.5 percent in the recession year of 1992. Once the economy recovered, though, the jobless rate started to drop. By 1999, only 4.2 percent of workers did not have a job. It was the lowest rate in thirty years.

The United States seemed to have weathered the economic problems of the 1970s and 1980s. It still had the largest economy in the world—by far. As the table on page 68 shows, the American GDP was larger than those of the second and third largest economies combined. GDP is gross domestic product, the total value of all goods and services produced and sold within a country.

Most remarkably, the economy generated a huge number of jobs. In 1980, just under 100 million people had jobs. By the late 1990s, that number had grown to more than 130 million. Despite all the gloomy news for many years, then, the 1990s seemed to show a highly successful economy.

Still, there were some troubling signs. One problem was the growing gulf between rich and poor Americans. In the 1980s and 1990s, the wealthiest families saw their income go up at a much higher rate than poorer families. In 1992, 90 percent of all Americans controlled only 61 percent of the nation's total income. That was down seven points from 1980.

Another troubling sign was the steep drop in the amount of money Americans saved. In 1975, Americans saved 9 percent of their income. That rate fell steadily until, by 1999, they were saving only 2.2 percent—just over two cents of every dollar. Some people simply did not earn enough to save. Others had to dip into their savings in order to get by. At the same time, consumers were borrowing more than ever before. Some consumers used credit cards to buy luxury items or to travel. Some needed them just to meet regular expenses or medical emergencies. For some, the mountain of debt proved disastrous when they lost their jobs and could not meet credit payments. Throughout the 1990s, a growing number of people had to declare bankruptcy—meaning they could not pay off their debts.

Another problem was the country's soaring trade deficit. The value of the goods the country imported was larger than the value of its exports. Throughout the 1980s and 1990s, Americans bought more foreign goods than the nation sold to other countries. Some economists said that these trade deficits weakened the American economy. Because of the deficits, foreigners held a large supply of American dollars. Others said there was nothing wrong with that. The foreigners would simply invest those dollars in the United States by buying land or companies. Then it would be in their interest to help the American economy grow so that the investments would pay off.

It's a Small World, After All

While this debate raged, one fact became clear. The economies of the world were increasingly tied together. The United States had long supported the goal of free trade—the removal of barriers to trade between countries. The aim was to create new markets abroad for American products. In many ways, the strategy worked. American exports increased eleven times from 1960 to 1980, from $20 billion to $220 billion. By the end of the century, they had soared to nearly $700 billion. American blue jeans, cigarettes, and cola drinks became popular around the world. McDonald's enjoyed amazing success, spreading to 120 countries and serving around 40 million customers a day. American television shows, movies, singers, and athletes gained worldwide success. Basketball star Michael Jordan became world famous, and people in Africa and China eagerly bought jerseys with his number.

Of course, globalization—the growing interdependence of the world's economies—cut both ways. Free trade also gave Americans more access to goods made abroad—and they were happy to buy them. Nowhere was the change more evident than in the auto industry. In the 1950s and 1960s, American car makers enjoyed boom times. In 1960, the Big Three American auto companies—General Motors, Ford, and Chrysler—sold 92 out of every 100 cars bought in the United States. But these companies suffered two major blows in the 1970s. The oil crisis raised the demand for cars that used less gasoline. Since few American cars qualified, consumers began to buy cars made in Japan and Germany. The second jolt was a decline in the quality of American-made cars.

The World's Largest Economies, 1998

	COUNTRY	GDP (billions of dollars)
1.	United States	$8,511
2.	China	4,420
3.	Japan	2,903
4.	Germany	1,813
5.	India	1,689
6.	France	1,320
7.	United Kingdom	1,252
8.	Italy	1,181
9.	Brazil	1,035
10.	Mexico	815

Source: CIA World Factbook

American automakers watched their share of the car market shrink each year.

They changed to become more competitive—and it worked. In the 1980s, they built more cars that burned less gasoline than before. (In the 1990s, the car makers sold more trucks and heavier cars that guzzled gas. But the fuel crisis was over by then, and the public bought the cars gladly.) U.S. manufacturers improved the quality of their cars. Still, the big automakers faced a new world. By the late 1990s, cars made abroad accounted for 53 of every 100 cars bought each year in the United States. However, half of those 53 cars were manufactured in Canada or Mexico in plants owned by American car companies. So the figure was not quite as bad as it looked.

On the other hand, Japanese and German car companies had their own factories in the United States. And those factories built cars that cut into American car sales. And one of the Big Three was no longer an American company. In 1998, the German car company Daimler-Benz merged with Chrysler. While the new company was supposed to be an equal partnership between the two firms, German executives dominated it.

Auto sales were just part of a growing problem between the United States and Japan. During the 1970s and 1980s, the United States developed a huge trade deficit with Japan. There were two reasons. First, American consumers bought growing numbers of Japanese cars—and televisions, videocassette recorders, stereos, cameras, computers, and other electronic equipment. Second, Japan blocked American companies from selling their goods in Japan. The American government tried to convince Japan to loosen those trade barriers. But the trade deficit continued to soar. Japan was not the only Asian economy that created problems for the United States. In the late 1980s and 1990s, the Chinese economy passed Japan to become the world's second largest. Throughout these years, the United States imported more and more goods from China. Its trade deficit with that country soared. By the middle 1990s, it had reached more than $30 billion a year.

The American effort to convince Japan to drop trade barriers was part of a larger movement taking place around the world. Countries were signing trade agreements that linked their economies. The largest of these trade blocs was the European Community, which included 15 members in Western Europe. These countries agreed to break down trade barriers for each other's goods. In the process, they created one of the world's largest markets. Most of the countries even agreed to use a common currency. They dropped their old national money systems in favor of a new euro.

American leaders grew concerned that a unified European market could become a major economic competitor. So they began to push for a regional trade bloc in North America. The result was the North American Free Trade Agreement (NAFTA), signed by the United States, Mexico, and Canada. The plan called for the three countries to cut down all trade barriers for each other. In 1991, President George Bush predicted that NAFTA would bring great benefits to American workers:

> I don't have to tell anyone about Mexico's market potential: 85 million consumers who want to buy our goods. Nor do I have to tell you that as Mexico grows and prospers, it will need even more of the goods we're best at producing: computers, manufacturing equipment, high-tech and high-value products.

Not everyone agreed. Labor unions said that open trade with Mexico would lead to the loss of even more American jobs. But when Bill Clinton was elected president in 1992, he supported NAFTA, too. In 1993, Congress voted to approve the trade treaty. The effects were immediate. American exports to Mexico did rise—but imports from Mexico rose even faster. Until 1994, the United States had enjoyed a trade surplus with Mexico. Starting in 1995, America imported far more goods from Mexico than it sold there. By 1999, the American trade deficit with Mexico reached nearly $23 billion.

While American workers might have suffered from these changes, American companies were thriving. Huge corporations like General Electric, General Motors, Ford, Exxon, IBM, Wal-

In 1994, the U.S. Congress approved the North American Free Trade Agreement (NAFTA). The agreement helped encourage American businesses to open factories south of the border in Mexico where wages are lower. Many Americans, especially members of labor unions, opposed NAFTA for this reason. (Library of Congress)

Mart, and Mobil still ranked among the largest corporations in the world. Indeed, nearly a third of the world's top 500 corporations were American. With operations in many countries, it did not matter if their American workforce got smaller. General Motors shipped fewer than 100,000 American-made cars to other countries in a year. Yet it had nearly $50 billion in sales outside the United States. It simply made the cars in other countries.

The growing globalization had its critics. Some people charged that the giant multinational corporations no longer had any loyalty to their home countries. They were only interested in making money and would do anything to achieve that goal, even if it meant going against the interests of their original national home. Critics said that the multinationals took unfair advantage of people in poor countries by paying them low wages and forcing them to work in unpleasant factories. They said that the multinationals moved to poorer countries so they could avoid laws limiting pollution. And, they said, the multinationals were destroying the unique cultures of the world by making every place look the same.

The criticism reached a peak in 1999. That year, the World Trade Organization (WTO) met in Seattle, Washington. The WTO—which counted most countries as members—aimed to promote world trade. But critics said that WTO actions simply made it easier for multinationals to take over the world's economy. When the trade ministers of scores of countries gathered in Seattle for the 1999 WTO meeting, they were met by protesters. An estimated 50,000 activists took to the streets. They chanted slogans and staged demonstrations against globalization and multinational companies.

Supporters of globalization countered the criticisms. They said that global companies helped spread ideas of human dignity and democratic values. They granted that the wages paid to factory workers in Malaysia or Mexico were lower than those paid in the United States or Western Europe. But they pointed out that those workers were still better off than others in their countries. As economist Paul Krugman said, "To claim that [these workers] have been impoverished by globalization . . . you have to forget that those workers were even poorer before . . . and ignore the fact that those who do not have access to global markets are far worse off than those who do." Whatever the arguments, globalization was happening, and very quickly.

Wall Street Wonders

While economic news was being made all over the world, much of it came out of Wall Street, the New York home of American financial markets. Stocks and bonds were bought and sold there. When investors buy stock, they buy part ownership in a corporation. When they buy bonds, they are, in effect, lending the corporation money. All that buying and selling made several headlines in the 1980s and 1990s.

In the early 1980s, the bond markets were busier than the stock market. In those years, interest rates were high. That meant that people could make more money from bonds than they could from stocks. About 1984, though, stocks began to look better as an investment, and the stock market began to rise. The Dow Jones Industrial Average tracks the value of a select group of important stocks, which shows overall trends in the market. The Dow jumped more than 300 points from 1984 to 1985 and another 300 by 1986—and it kept climbing. Investors were jubilant—until "Black Monday." On Monday, October 19, 1987, so many people sold stock that the Dow fell 508 points. It was the biggest one-day drop in history, as stocks lost nearly a fifth of their value. Fortunately, the market rallied over the next few days.

The 1987 stock market crash was a jolt to investors' confidence, but only a brief one. The market began to rise again, and did so steadily—and sharply—throughout the 1990s. New record highs were set at a dizzying pace, and the Dow Jones average eventually passed the 11,000 mark, a fivefold increase over the level in 1988. Three factors fueled this surge. First, the economy was growing faster than it had in the 1980s. Second, the federal government was showing budget surpluses—taking in more money than it spent. That increased confidence in the economy and drove interest rates down, making stocks more attractive than bonds. Third, the rise in Internet use was attracting new, and exciting, business opportunities. Many companies—called "dot-coms" for their World Wide Web domain name—formed in the 1990s to make money off the Internet. To get the funds to grow, they offered stock to the public. The initial stock sales generated millions for the company's owners. Later stock trading drove prices up even higher, making millions—on paper—for many people.

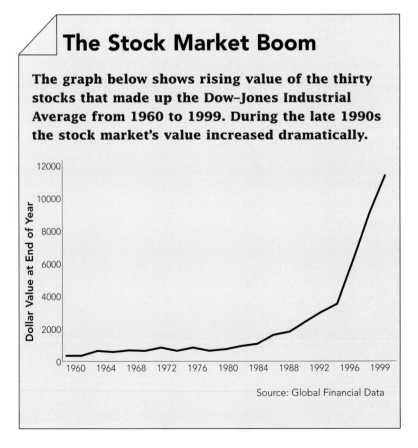

The Stock Market Boom

The graph below shows rising value of the thirty stocks that made up the Dow–Jones Industrial Average from 1960 to 1999. During the late 1990s the stock market's value increased dramatically.

Source: Global Financial Data

Not everyone was thrilled with the 1990s stock boom. Alan Greenspan warned that the soaring stock prices might reveal too much optimism. In 1996, he spoke of "irrational exuberance"—that is, investors letting their emotions get the better of their judgment. As stock prices continued to soar, many experts thought Greenspan was being too gloomy. After the turn of the century, the stock market fell far and fast. Then the old economist looked pretty smart.

During the 1990s, though, the stock market still looked attractive. It began to attract more people than ever before. In the past, most Americans looked on Wall Street trading as an interesting diversion but something remote from their lives. That changed in the late 1900s. By the late 1990s, 52 percent of all Americans—more than one out of every two—owned stock. As late as 1980, the rate had only been 13 percent, or one out of every eight people. The main spur to this growth was the spread of retirement funds. These are funds that people invest in during their working years. Then, when they retire, the money is available to meet living expenses. Many companies set up retirement funds for their workers. In most cases, employers matched some money contributed by workers. As the stock market kept rising, the funds owned by many people rose in value.

New Winners and Losers

Business is a competitive world, with winners and losers. Some of those winners in the 1980s and 1990s were familiar names. These companies had dominated business for much of the century. General Electric thrived under the dynamic leadership of Jack Welch. Ford rebounded from troubled times to challenge General Motors as the leading car company. Oil companies remained successful. Boeing, the aircraft manufacturer, was another highly successful company—although it was increasingly challenged by foreign airplane makers.

Some of the winners in the late 1990s were newcomers. One of these was retailer Wal-Mart. Founder Sam Walton's idea was to create huge stores that sold a great variety of products at very low prices. He did it by setting up giant warehouses that could feed several stores. Because his warehouses were so large, he could buy goods in large quantities at low prices. He passed those savings on to consumers. He also located his stores in rural areas, where there was little competition. The strategy worked, and Wal-Mart became the nation's largest retailer. In fact, it became one of the country's largest companies—only General Motors had higher sales. Wal-Mart was also one of the country's largest employers, with nearly one million workers. Falling far behind were traditional retail giants like Sears, J.C. Penneys, and department stores.

Other successful retailers followed the same strategy of selling goods at a high discount. Target and Kmart, like Wal-Mart, sold everything. Most of the discounters, though, specialized in a small range of goods. Toys R Us became the leading toy retailer. Home Depot and Lowe's led the "do-it-yourself" market. They set up large stores where people could buy hardware, paint, flooring, doors, windows, and anything else they wanted to fix up their homes. Best Buy and Circuit City sold consumer electronics, music, and movies. Barnes & Noble opened giant bookstores and welcomed browsers by decorating them with comfortable easy chairs and coffee service.

New companies also arose in the phone industry. AT&T had dominated the telephone business for years, doing everything from making phones to handling local and long distance calls. Then the government sued the company, charging that it was a trust that unfairly limited competition. In the early 1980s, a judge agreed and ordered the phone giant to be split into several different companies. Local service would be handled by seven regional phone companies, which were nicknamed "Baby Bells." AT&T would be allowed to sell long distance, but it also had to accept competition. Soon, new phone companies sprang up, with Sprint and MCI emerging as the strongest competitors against AT&T for long distance business.

The AT&T case broke up one of America's largest corporations, but the main trend in the 1980s and 1990s was for enlarging. Some of the growth came in the personal computer industry, which was born and flourished in this period. The biggest winner here was Microsoft, which produced software for the great majority of personal computers. Microsoft founder Bill Gates had signed an agreement with IBM to provide the operating system, the basic software, for the new personal computer it released in 1981. High sales of IBM computers—and the machines made by other companies that worked the same way—brought growing streams of revenue to Microsoft. The company branched out, creating programs for word processing and other business functions. In 1995, it launched a whole new operating system—Windows 95—in a worldwide party. By then, 90 percent of the world's computers were running on Microsoft software. The company sold nearly $20 billion worth of products a year by the end of the decade. Gates became one of the richest men in the world.

Microsoft was late getting into the Internet business, but once it did, it jumped in with a vengeance. The government then sued the company, charging that Microsoft had broken antitrust laws in trying to enter this market. A judge agreed with the government, and threatened to break the company up. But Microsoft appealed the decision to a higher court, and the judges there overturned that part of the judge's decision. Microsoft remained a giant.

The companies that made computers grew large as well. IBM actually dropped out of the personal computer business. Like Microsoft, newcomers Dell, Sun Systems, and Gateway were led by daring and smart founders. They started out small but grew to be major players. Internet companies like America Online and Yahoo! helped make the World Wide Web popular by giving people ways of connecting and moving through the mass of information. Amazon revolutionized retailing by creating an easy-to-use system for buying books online. It helped give birth to "e-commerce," or the buying of goods online. By the end of the decade, Internet sales totaled about $300 billion—nearly the same level as auto sales.

Bill Gates, founder and chairman of Microsoft Corporation
(Courtesy of Microsoft, Inc.)

The trend to bigness was seen in several mergers, or agreements to join companies together. Each year, it seemed, a new record was set for these deals. In 1994, AT&T bought a cell-phone company for $16.7 billion. Two years later, Walt Disney bought Capital Cities/ABC for $18.3 billion. In 1997, Bell Atlantic—one of the "Baby Bells"—acquired Nynex—another "Baby Bell"—for $30.8 billion. The next year, Travelers, an insurance business, bought Citicorp, a banking company, for a whopping $72.6 billion. The record was hit in 1999, when oil giant Exxon bought oil giant Mobil for $86.4 billion.

Some of the mergers aimed to achieve what executives called "synergies." This was especially the case in the joining of media companies, such as Disney and Capital Cities/ABC. Disney brought movies, music, and theme parks to the deal. Capital Cities/ABC had record companies, a television network, and various cable networks. These provided ways for Disney to get its movies and music to the public. Business leaders hoped to make deals between the different divisions of the new company that would hold down costs and let everyone share in the profits. At the same time, media companies were finding new ways to make money. Popular movies or television shows were exploited in new ways. The companies that owned them signed deals with toy companies, video-game makers, clothing firms, and fast-food restaurants. An avalanche of products hit the market.

The goal of many of these new mega-corporations was to reach into new businesses and to make operations more efficient. One way of achieving efficiency was to cut duplication—the number of similar products or services offered. There was plenty of that. The newly formed giants often had people in more than one place doing the same kind of work—work that earlier had been done for two different companies. So the big mergers were often followed by layoffs, as once-valuable workers were no longer needed. Corporate executives said they were "trimming fat from the payroll" and "cutting redundant operations." Wall Street investors applauded them for making "tough decisions" because profits rose. Meanwhile, tens of thousands of people suddenly found themselves without jobs. That was just one of the ways that the workplace changed in the 1980s and 1990s.

Chapter Five

Work

American businesses underwent many changes in the late 1900s. As a result, work changed in many ways, too. The two chief changes had to do with technology and the increasing competition brought on by globalization. New technologies made it possible to work faster—and at all hours. And the intense competition brought about changes in how companies were organized and in how work was done.

Technology in the Workplace

The biggest change in workplace technology was the spread of the personal computer (PC). In 1980, workers still relied on typewriters and telephones. Reports had to be dictated or written out by hand and then laboriously typed, proofread, and corrected. The largest companies had computers, but these were generally large machines that were controlled by a highly skilled group of workers. Most employees did not have direct access to the data on these systems. Getting information could take days.

Computers changed all that. By the late 1990s, most office workers in most companies had computers on their desks. Workers used word-processing programs to write, edit, format, and print reports and other documents. The final product could include photographs and other illustrations, in full color. They looked far more professional than anything that came out of the

Office workers (LEFT) **gather to discuss business** (Photodisc). **Although most firefighters are men, some women have also joined firefighting companies, like this one** (RIGHT) **in New York City.** (Library of Congress)

typewriter era. Workers used electronic spreadsheets to make complex financial calculations. They could tap into the company's database of facts about products, services, and employees. With e-mail, they could quickly send messages to coworkers and clients. With Internet connections, they could tap into a wealth of information.

Business writers predicted that the new machines would bring about the "paperless office." That is, all work would be done and stored on a computer. There would no longer be a need for cumbersome paper files. While the paperless office never appeared, the spread of computers did revolutionize work. Employees who had more access to more information could make faster—and better—decisions. They could be more helpful when customers called in to ask about products or to check on the status of an order. Lightweight laptop computers kept sales workers who were always on the road in close contact with the home office.

But PCs changed more than just office work. Stores replaced cash registers with computer-driven machines. Now cashiers aimed lasers at the special bar codes imprinted on packages or tags. The code identified the product and instantly entered its price onto the computer.

This system was first used in supermarkets, but it quickly spread to many different kinds of stores. The new system gave stores several benefits. First, customer checkouts went more quickly and more accurately. Cashiers no longer had to input strings of numbers—which took away the chance of a cashier making an error. Second, stores could change prices and not have to worry about the cashier entering an old price. Whatever price was stored at that moment in the store's central computer was the price charged to the customer. Third, stores were able to keep an up-to-the-minute record of their inventory, or the supply of items they had for sale. Each time a customer bought a new pair of jeans, say, the store's database subtracted a pair—of the right brand and size—from the computer's record. In this way, purchasing workers could see when stocks in some items were falling low and order more.

Even manufacturing took to computers. Engineers began to use sophisticated programs to design new products. Some factories installed computer-driven robots on their assembly lines. The new machines became the new factory workers. They built the products. These complex robots cost a lot of money but provided many benefits. Robotic painters could be programmed to apply a certain amount of paint, holding down costs by never putting on too much. They never tired, which meant that quality could be upheld. And they could do work—like welding or painting—that was dangerous to workers' health.

Other workers found new ways to use computers. Busy people used tiny machines to store their schedules and the names and phone numbers of their key clients. Auto mechanics used computers so they could see if a car was working properly. Even farmers used computers. Some simply used them to handle their financial records. In the late 1900s, though, more and more came to use computers to decide such things as what crops to plant on what part of their fields and how much to fertilize.

Technology moved so quickly that some early machines of the period were virtually ignored later. In the 1980s, two changes made communications more rapid than ever. Federal Express created a new business based on the idea of guaranteed overnight

During the 1980s and 1990s, many factories, like this Honda automotive factory in Marysville, Ohio, began using robotic equipment to speed manufacturing. (Courtesy of Honda Motors)

delivery. Suddenly, workers in a New York company could send a report to people in a California company and know that the package would arrive by the next business morning. FedEx, as it came to be called, was born in the 1970s, but became highly successful in the 1980s. The next innovation made overnight delivery look slow. Facsimile (fax) machines used telephone lines to transmit images of the information on paper over long distances almost instantly. Now those New York workers could fax their report to California the same day. By the end of the 1990s, though, the Internet and e-mail had made even fax machines less necessary. Instead of printing out the report from their computer and then faxing it, a worker simply had to press a button to transmit the report by e-mail.

New Technologies Create New Problems

The spread of computerized technology raised new issues, though. Companies had to train their workers to use the new systems. New businesses sprang up to offer custom-made training sessions to large numbers of workers. The situation was complicated by the fight among the software companies to get more and more customers to buy their programs. Every few years, software publishers issued new versions of their programs. Each was an attempt to beat the competition by supplying more features that workers could use to do a greater variety of work. The result, though, was to create programs that grew harder to learn. They had to be relearned each time the company bought a new version.

Another problem was a health issue. Workers spent more and more time at a computer keyboard inputting information. As a result, some developed health problems. The most prominent was a problem in the hands called repetitive stress injury. The problem resulted from repeating the same motions over and over again for long periods of time day after day. This repetition caused swelling in tendons in the wrist and hands. The swollen tendons then put pressure on a nerve, which brought pain. That pain could be severe. Doctors found some ways to treat the condition. In some cases, though, workers needed surgery. And some workers had to find new jobs to get away from the repeated work that caused the problem.

Privacy also became an issue. In the 1990s, workers came to rely increasingly on e-mail for communication. Just as workers had

Henry Ford and Mass Production

The rise in American industrial productivity in the 1920s owed much to mass-production techniques developed by car-maker Henry Ford a decade earlier. Mass production—using standard parts, and assembling them into a finished product in a series of steps—was nothing new in American industry. Ford, however, turned mass production into a science.

In Ford plants, car parts rolled down a waist-high, chain-driven assembly line. Each worker "on the line" performed a single operation—fitting a carburetor, for example, or spray-painting a hood. At the end of the line, a finished car rolled off. Ford refined the process so finely that by the mid-1920s his Highland Park plant in Detroit could produce a Model T in just under six hours. Other carmakers adopted Ford's methods, and soon mass-production techniques took hold in other industries.

In 1914, Henry Ford stunned the nation by announcing that he would pay his workers $5.00 for an eight-hour workday—a wage he raised to $6.00 per day in 1919. Five dollars a day was about twice the average wage for factory workers at the time.

Ford wasn't offering his employees high wages out of generosity. He needed to pay well to keep assembly-line workers from quitting after a few weeks or months on the job. Worn out by the pace many did quit before the introduction of the $5.00 day.

The problem was that by turning mass production into a science, Ford essentially turned workers into machines. Ford's assembly-line workers found it hard to take any pride or satisfaction in their work when all they did was perform a series of simple motions, over and over again, hour after hour, day after day.

And while the work wasn't particularly hard physically, keeping up with the line was stressful. It ruined even the simple pleasures of working life, like lunch: One Ford worker recalled that "to transfer [food] to the stomach in fifteen minutes without choking, and still have time to wipe the crumbs from one's mouth before the production bell sounds again is an exact science made possible only by the application of Ford production principles."

Henry Ford (LEFT), with Thomas Edison (SECOND FROM LEFT), President Warren Harding (SITTING, THIRD FROM LEFT) and others on a camping trip. (Library of Congress)

Ford Motor Company's "Service Department" was responsible for stopping the unions from being organized among Ford workers. Sometimes, the group used violence to intimidate union leaders. In this photograph, members of the Service Department approach United AutoWorkers leaders on the overpass outside the Ford plant in River Rouge, Michigan. Seconds later members of the department assaulted the UAW activists in what became known as the Battle of the Overpass. (Library of Congress)

they kept food packages out of the plants. This led to violent clashes between strikers, police, and GM "security forces." The governor of Michigan considered ordering the National Guard to force the strikers from the plants. But Lewis persuaded him that this would only lead to more and worse violence.

Finally, after forty-four days, GM gave in and recognized the UAW. It was a stunning victory for Lewis and the CIO in particular and for organized labor in general.

The sit-down strike proved a powerful new weapon in labor's arsenal. By mid-1937, almost a half-million American workers took part in sit-down strikes at hundreds of businesses.

The Ford Motor Company, however, held out against the UAW. Henry Ford was still in charge. He was a firm foe of any union organizing efforts.

In May 1936, fifty UAW organizers gathered at a road overpass leading to the Ford plant at River Rouge, Michigan. They were there to pass out pro-union leaflets. Although the organizers had a permit, "service men" from Ford's private police force tried to chase them away. When UAW leader Walter Reuther and his colleagues held their ground, the "service men" beat them up. Several organizers were badly hurt.

Newspaper photographs of the bloodied victims of the "Battle of the Overpass" won much public support for the UAW. Still, it took five more years and much pressure from the federal government before Ford was fully unionized.

The Little Steel Strike

The next battleground for the CIO was the steel industry. The Steel Workers Organizing Committee (SWOC) began to organize both "Big Steel" (the United States Steel Corporation) and its smaller competitors, which together were known as "Little Steel."

Big Steel fell without a fight. After Lewis met with the head of United States Steel in January 1937, the corporation agreed to collective bargaining with the SWOC. Lewis expected Little Steel to do the same. Instead, the owners of all but one of the Little Steel companies opposed the SWOC. In May, the SWOC called a strike and 85,000 steelworkers walked out of Little Steel plants in seven states.

Republic Steel kept its South Chicago, Illinois, plant operating by bringing in strikebreakers. These were known to union supporters as "scabs." When strikers set up a picket line to keep the strikebreakers out of the plant, Chicago police used force to push back the picketing strikers.

On May 30—Memorial Day—about 1,000 strikers, union supporters, and their family members marched to the Republic plant to form a picket line. About 200 police blocked their path. What happened next is still unclear, but the police began firing on the crowd. First they fired tear gas, then bullets. When the smoke cleared, forty marchers had been shot. Ten died, and many more were injured.

The "Memorial Day Massacre" was the most deadly episode during the Little Steel Strike. But it wasn't the only one. Elsewhere, as many as sixteen people died in clashes between strikers and strikebreakers and security forces.

The strike dragged on. Soon many strikers and their families were hungry and broke. Finally, in July, the SWOC called off the strike. Even under pressure from the National Labor Relations Board, Little Steel refused to fully accept unions until 1942.

The Fair Labor Standard Act

The failure of the Little Steel Strike was a setback for labor. But it was more than balanced by the huge gains unions made between 1934 and 1940. During those years, more than 7 million Americans joined unions. By 1940, a third of all workers enjoyed union representation. And between 1937 and 1940, the NLRB oversaw union elections at more than 3,000 workplaces.

Just as important, labor's struggle in the 1930s led the federal government to help improve conditions for American workers outside unions. In 1938, Congress passed the Fair Labor Standards Act. The law established a minimum wage at forty cents per hour. It set the standard workweek at forty hours. Hours worked over that limit had to be paid as overtime.

The Fair Labor Standards Act didn't apply to everyone. It did not include farm laborers, for example. But it helped millions of working people enjoy a little more of what John L. Lewis called "American economic sunlight."

Chapter Six

Religion

Lawyer Clarence Darrow (LEFT) defended Tennessee science teacher John Scopes in the famous "Monkey Trial." Scopes had taught the theory of evolution, which states that human beings are descended from apes. According to Tennessee law at the time, it was illegal to teach Evolution. Many Fundamentalist Christians, including members of the this Pentacostal Prophecy Tabernacle near Modesto, California, (RIGHT), believed that evolution contradicted the teachings of the Bible. (Library of Congress)

On the surface, America in the 1920s and 1930s was a very religious society. The existence of God was taken for granted by almost all Americans, and a majority of the population claimed to belong to some form of organized religion.

Religion played a big part in the lives of many American communities. Ministers, priests, and rabbis were often important figures, sought after for advice and opinions on the issues of the day. Newspapers regularly printed church sermons and religious articles. Children in many public schools began the day with a prayer, or even a reading from the Bible.

At the same time, religion did not necessarily take up a large part of most people's lives. For example, researchers found that many more people claimed to belong to various churches than actually showed up regularly for services.

America's Religions, 1921–1940

Whether or not they attended church services regularly, most Americans in the 1920s and 1930s considered themselves Christians. Although the largest single denomination (church group) in the country was the Roman Catholic Church, two-thirds of American Christians were Protestants.

There was a wide variety of Protestant denominations, ranging from the "mainstream" churches (Episcopal, Baptist, Methodist, and so on), each with millions of members, to hundreds of smaller denominations and individual churches and not associated with a particular denomination.

Although most of the "mainstream" Protestant churches had members everywhere in the country, certain denominations had big concentrations of members in particular regions. Baptists and Methodists, for example, were most common in the South and Midwest, while the Congregational and Unitarian churches were strongest in New England. Members of the Church of Jesus Christ of Latter-Day Saints, often called Mormons, formed the majority of the population in Utah.

Many denominations, too, were associated with particular ethnic groups. Eastern Orthodox churches could be found in any community where Greek and Russian immigrants had settled, for example. There were many Lutherans in the upper Midwest, a region that was home to many people of German and Scandinavian background.

As with so much of American life in the 1920a and 1930s, religion was also divided along racial lines. All but a small percentage of African Americans—almost all of whom were Protestants—worshipped in churches of their own. Many African Americans belonged to denominations like the African Methodist Episcopal (AME) Church, but most were members of small independent churches. Even those African Americans who belonged to the "mainstream" Baptist and Methodist denominations usually had to worship apart from whites.

Apart from Christianity, the only major religion with many followers in America during this era was Judaism. There were 3.5 million American Jews in 1920. Most of them lived in the big cities of the Northeast. Almost half of the nation's Jewish population lived in New York City.

The exact number of American Buddhists and Muslims during this period isn't known, but their numbers were small. The religious makeup of America didn't change very much between 1920 and 1940. In this era, most Americans tended to stay with the faith of their parents and to raise their own children in that faith.

Fundamentalism versus Liberalism

The most important development in American Christianity during the 1920s was the growth of Fundamentalism.

During the nineteenth century, advances in science led some Christians to question long-held beliefs that were based on a literal reading of the Bible. For example, according to the Bible's Book of Genesis, God created the Earth in seven days. The new science of geology, however, seemed to show that the earth had been formed by natural forces acting over millions of years.

The Theory of Evolution, especially, sparked a controversy within Christianity. In 1859, British scientist Charles Darwin published *On the Origin of Species*. In it, he presented his theory that living creatures evolve (develop) over a very long time through a process he called natural selection. This theory contradicted the Bible on several levels. Most troubling to many Christians was the fact that if Darwin's theory was true, it meant that humans had evolved from animals, instead of being uniquely created by God.

Some Christians believed that science and religion could coexist. This movement came to be called Liberal Theology. (Theology is an organized system of religious belief.) Leaders of this movement, especially the Baptist minister Harry Emerson Fosdick, argued that the Bible did not have to be taken as the literal word of God. In their view, what was really important in the Christian faith remained important whether or not the world was created in seven days or over seventy million years.

Fundamentalism versus Modernism

The Fundamentalist movement gained many followers in the 1920s and 1930s, especially in the South and the Midwest. In some denominations, like the Southern Baptists, Fundamentalists became the majority. Other denominations were split into Fundamentalist and Liberal camps, and new denominations, like the Independent Fundamental Churches of America, were established.

The growth of Fundamentalism led to a controversy that attracted the attention of all Americans.

The 1920s was a time of rapid change in American society. Jazz music, Hollywood movies, new roles for women, new ideas about sex and relationships—all these things made many Americans uncomfortable. A sizeable part of the population—not all of them Fundamentalist Protestants—believed that the nation's traditional values were threatened by Modernism.

Fundamentalists and other like-minded Americans also resented the fact that many Modernist writers and intellectuals disrespected their beliefs and made fun of them.

There wasn't much the Fundamentalists could do to halt the spread of new ideas, but there was one area in which they could challenge the Modernists—the teaching of the Theory of Evolution in public schools. The challenge was laid down at the World's Fundamentalist Convention at Fort Worth, Texas, in 1924. The convention passed a resolution that called on states "to force all teachers to sign...a statement of creed [belief] which affirms a firm and steadfast faith in the Genesis account of creation...."

The following year, State Representative John Washington Butler sponsored a new law in the Tennessee Legislature: "An act prohibiting the teaching of Evolution Theory in all the Universities, Normals [teacher's colleges], and all other public schools of the State."

"The evolutionist who denies the Biblical story of creation, as well as other Biblical accounts, cannot be called a Christian," Butler said, "[Evolution] goes hand in hand with Modernism... robs the Christian of his hope and undermines the foundation of our government...."

The move to outlaw the teaching of evolution was not just a matter of whether the theory was right or wrong. Public education in America has always been paid for by taxpayers. Opponents of evolution felt that it was wrong for taxpayers' dollars to support the teaching of something that the majority of people in the community considered offensive. The anti-evolution law passed Tennessee's legislature in a 71-5 vote. This set the stage for one of the most dramatic court cases of the era: the Scopes Trial.

Pentecostalism

Another movement within American Christianity, Pentecostalism, also won many followers in the 1920s.

Pentecostalism took its name from Pentecost, an event described in the Book of Acts in the Christian New Testament. According to Acts, Jesus Christ's disciples (followers) were gathered a week after he had risen from the dead, when "Suddenly a sound like the blowing of a violent wind came from heaven and filled

Evolution on Trial

To the American Civil Liberties Union (ACLU), Tennessee's 1925 ban on teaching evolution was ban of free speech. ACLU lawyers asked John T. Scopes, a young teacher in Dayton, Tennessee, to teach evolution in his high school classroom. This would lead to his arrest and a trial in a state court, which the ACLU hoped would eventually lead to the anti-evolution law being declared unconstitutional.

Scopes agreed to the plan, was arrested and released on bail, and a trial date was set for July 1925. Roger Baldwin of the ACLU announced that "We shall take the Scopes case to the Supreme Court if necessary to establish that a teacher may tell the truth without being thrown in jail." Clarence Darrow, a brilliant lawyer well known for defending controversial figures, agreed to defend Scopes.

William Jennings Bryan agreed to help the prosecution—the state of Tennessee—in the case. Bryan was one of the most famous figures of the era. A three-time candidate for president, he was known for champ-ioning the interests of poor and rural Amer-icans against those of the rich and powerful.

Bryan was also a Fundamentalist. He told evolutionists that "You believe in the age of rocks. I believe in the Rock of Ages."

When the trial began, thousands of curious people swelled Dayton's population, hundreds packed the courtroom, and millions more listened to the trial by radio. Vendors sold souvenirs, bands played, and various groups paraded in support of one side or the other. (The case quickly became known as the "Monkey Trial" because the Theory of Evolution held that humans had evolved from "lower orders" of animals, including primates.)

For five days, lawyers and experts debated. Then Darrow called Bryan himself to the witness stand. For two hours Darrow grilled Bryan about his religious beliefs, often sarcastically. By the time the judge ended the questioning, Darrow had made Bryan appear confused and even foolish. According to one reporter, "Darrow never spared him. It was masterful, but it was pitiful."

The trial ended in a guilty verdict for Scopes, which everyone expected. He had, after all, clearly broken the law. The judge, however, fined Scopes only $100. Five days later Bryan, exhausted by the trial, died in his sleep.

In 1926 a Tennessee appeals court threw out the verdict—not on the basis that the anti-evolution law was unconstitutional, but on a technicality: It was up to the jury, not the judge, to set the fine. The law stayed on the books.

After trial, a number of states passed laws requiring that the Bible's account of creation, which came to be known as Creation Science, be taught along with evolution in public schools. In 1988 the U.S. Supreme Court ruled that teaching Creation Science violated the separation of church and state established by the Constitution's First Amendment. Some states and communities, however, have challenged the ruling. The many issues raised by the "Monkey Trial"—religion versus science, freedom of speech in the classroom, state authority over education —are still being debated today.

the whole house where they were sitting. They saw what seemed to be tongues of fire that separated and came to rest on each of them. All of them were filled with the Holy Spirit and began to speak in other tongues as the Spirit enabled them" (King James Bible, Acts 2:1–4).

In 1900, Charles Parham began to teach about this "baptism in the Holy Spirit" at Bethany Bible College in Topeka, Kansas. Six years later, one of Parham's students, an African American minister named William J. Seymour, took over a church at 312 Azusa Street in Los Angeles, California. Over the next three years Seymour's church became the center of a Pentecostal "revival" that would spread across America and, eventually, much of the world.

Unlike the Fundamentalists and Liberals, the Pentecostal, or "Holiness," movement was more concerned with the individual's experience of the "Holy Spirit" than with how to interpret the words of the Bible.

Pentecostal services were intense and emotional, very different from the more formal, serious worship common in most Protestant churches. Worshippers felt that the same spirit that had entered Jesus' disciples at the original Pentecost filled them. Besides "speaking in tongues," Pentecostalists believed the "gifts of the Spirit" included the ability to prophesy (foresee the future) and to heal the sick.

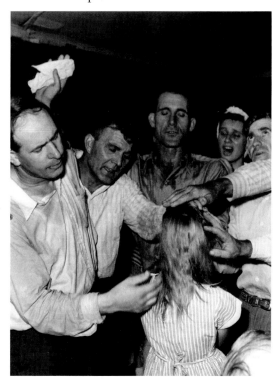

Although the "mainstream" Protestant denominations mostly rejected Pentecostalism, the movement gained millions of followers. New Pentecostalist denominations, like the Assemblies of God, were established, but most Pentecostalists belonged to small, independent churches.

Pentecostalism proved especially strong in the Depression years. By some estimates, the membership of Pentecostalist churches grew by about 50 percent in the 1930s, while "mainstream" Protestant churches lost about 10 percent of their membership.

A healing "laying on of hands" ceremony in the Pentecostal Church of God in Lejunior, Kentucky. (Library of Congress)

The Evangelists

Another feature of religious life in the 1920s were itinerant evangelists who traveled the country preaching and seeking converts to Christianity.

These evangelists included many colorful characters, like Billy Sunday, formerly a hard-drinking baseball player (he had played outfield for the Chicago White Sox) who had found religion and dedicated his life to evangelism. Other evangelists dedicated themselves to converting members of different groups—there was a railroad evangelist, a businessman's evangelist, even a cowboy evangelist.

The most famous evangelist of the 1920s—and one of the most important religious figures of the era—was a woman named Aimee Semple McPherson. Tall, good-looking, and usually dressed in flowing white robes, McPherson had a spellbinding effect on worshippers. She founded a mission, the Foursquare Gospel, in Los Angeles in 1922. One young man who saw her preach and who went on to become a famous actor said later that McPherson was "the most magnetic personality I was ever to encounter."

By 1923 McPherson—now known as "Sister Aimee"—moved the Foursquare Gospel into a specially constructed $1.5 million Angelus Temple, which could hold 5,000 worshippers. It was always overflowing.

Aimee Semple McPherson (Library of Congress)

In May 1926, McPherson disappeared. She was supposedly seen swimming in the Pacific Ocean, but a massive search found no trace of her. Wild rumors circulated about her fate. Three weeks later McPherson walked into a small town in Arizona. She claimed to have escaped from kidnappers. Her followers went wild with joy. More than 50,000 people met her train when she returned to Los Angeles. In a decade of sensational stories, this was one of the most sensational.

Soon, however, some people began to doubt her account. But McPherson stuck by her story, so what really happened will probably never be known. It hardly affected her popularity. She continued her work until her death in 1944. The Foursquare Gospel movement she started is still flourishing, and many later evangelists copied her methods with great success.

Roman Catholicism, 1920–1940

Although the Roman Catholic Church was the single largest Christian denomination in America during the 1920s and 1930s, Catholic Americans still faced misunderstanding and even outright prejudice during these decades.

Many native-born Americans, especially Fundamentalist Protestants, continued to view the Catholic Church as "the church of immigrants," and they believed that Catholics could never be "true Americans" as long as they owed allegiance to the Pope in Rome. Also, despite the fact that Catholics and Protestants shared many beliefs, the Catholic Church had customs that Protestants found difficult to understand or accept. For example, Catholic masses (services) were conducted in Latin rather than English during these decades. Also, the Catholic Church opposed Prohibition (see Chapter 2), while most Protestant churches supported it.

The split between Protestant and Catholic America was most visible in the presidential election of 1928. The Democratic candidate, New York Governor Al Smith, was Catholic. His Republican opponent, Secretary of Commerce Herbert Hoover was a member of the Society of Friends, or Quakers.

Smith's religion became a major issue in the campaign. In a small Delaware town, for example, local Republicans paid a Civil War veteran to tell voters that if Smith was elected, "The Pope is goin' to come over here ... and live in the White House and run the country." When Smith arrived in Oklahoma City to make a campaign speech, the Ku Klux Klan (see Chapter 2) met his train with flaming crosses.

Hoover won the election. Afterward, journalist Claude Bowers wrote that "The campaign of 1928 was the most disgraceful and threatening in our history up to that time. At some periods… waves of religious and racial intolerance had swept the country, but never had there been anything so widespread and sinister.…"

Prejudice and misunderstanding, however, sometimes worked both ways. During the 1920s and 1930s, some Catholic clergymen, like Father Charles Coughlin, the "radio priest" (see Chapter 2), preached their own brand of intolerance. Also, many Catholics were just as opposed to Modernism as the most diehard Protestant Fundamentalist. In 1934, for example, the Hollywood movie studios agreed to a Code of Decency, mostly because of pressure from Catholic leaders. It limited what could be shown on-screen.

Writing in the magazine *America Now* in the late 1930s, Catholic priest Francis X. Talbot summed up the often uneasy relationship between Catholic and non-Catholic America: "There is no blinking the fact that the non-Catholic American has as much difficulty in understanding the Catholic soul and spirit as the Catholic American has in [understanding] the minds and emotions of the non-Catholic citizen. The Catholic Church is forever being misunderstood and misjudged; and it is continually asserting itself in ways that give cause to new misjudgments.…"

American Judaism, 1920–1940

For American Jews, the 1920s and 1930s were a time of both progress and struggle. Jews from Russia, Poland, and other parts of Eastern Europe formed one of the largest immigrant groups in the decades just before and after the turn of the 20th century. By the late 1920s, after Congress largely halted immigration (see Chapter 2), most Jews in America were native-born.

Thanks in large part to a traditional respect for education, many Jews moved up the economic ladder rapidly, especially in the boom years of the 1920s. Jews became especially well represented in "white-collar" occupations like finance, medicine, education, and the law.

Nevertheless, American Jews in this era faced a level of anti-Semitic (anti-Jewish) feeling that's difficult to understand today.

Some of this prejudice had its basis in religion. America was an overwhelmingly Christian nation and many (though certainly not all) Protestant and Catholic Americans held an ancient, unreasonable grudge against Jews for what they believed was Jewish responsibility for Christ's death.

Other anti-Semites resented Jewish success and believed that Jews had become "too powerful" in fields like finance and the media. And some Americans disliked Jews just because they were a minority group whose religion and customs were different than those of the majority.

Anti-Semitism took many forms. Some of the nation's top universities admitted only small numbers of Jewish students (see Chapter 3) during this period. Some hospitals refused to hire Jewish doctors. And many apartment buildings, hotels, country clubs, resorts, and other facilities were "restricted"—a "polite" way of saying that Jews weren't welcome.

Sometimes anti-Semitism took even harsher forms. In 1920, carmaker Henry Ford, one of the most famous and influential figures of the era, began publishing a newspaper, *The Dearborn Independent*. The *Independent* ran anti-Semitic articles that were as nasty as they were ignorant. (Sample headline: "The Jewish Degradation of Baseball.")

A couple of years later, after much public protest, Ford told the *Independent*'s editor to "cut out the Jewish articles." By the standards of the time, Ford was a liberal in many ways—he believed women should have the right to vote, and he employed African Americans when many other businessmen wouldn't. The *Independent* episode, however, would always be a stain on his reputation.

In some ways, anti-Semitism became even worse in the 1930s. The fact that many socialist and communist leaders happened to be Jewish led extreme right-wing Americans to denounce Jews as "anti-American" radicals. Anti-Semitic foes of President Franklin Roosevelt also made much of the fact that most Jews supported the president, and that his cabinet and other advisers included several Jews.

New Movements

The United States has always been a fertile ground for new religious, spiritual, and self-improvement movements. This was certainly the case in the 1920s and 1930s.

Americans of this era joined movements that would be called "New Age" today. The World Unity Foundation, for example, which began in 1927, attracted many American intellectuals. The organization was devoted to creating "worldwide understanding and a humanized civilization" based on common elements in many worldwide religions.

America also produced some prophets of its own during these decades. One of the most famous was Father Divine, founder of the International Peace Mission Movement.

Little is known of Father Divine's early life beyond the fact that he was born George Baker and was a traveling preacher. By 1924 he was living on Long Island in New York State, where he attracted a tiny group of followers. They apparently came to believe that he was the personification of God. At some point he took the name Father M. J. Divine.

In 1924, Father Divine had some trouble with the local police, probably because he and most of his followers were African Americans in a mostly white community. (Father Divine preached the equality of all races, and his followers came to include many whites.) Soon afterward he moved his growing band of followers, now called the International Peace Mission Movement, to Harlem in New York City. From there the movement spread to other communities, mostly African American neighborhoods in big cities.

Father Divine was controversial. Members of more conventional faiths were uncomfortable with many of his teachings and the fact that his followers considered him to be, literally, divine. Critics also noted that Father Divine often made his followers turn their money and property over to him, and that he enjoyed luxuries. He reportedly drove a Rolls-Royce while demanding that his followers lead a simple lifestyle.

Nevertheless, Father Divine's movement gained many converts and admirers in the Depression because of the way its members weathered the hard times. The International Peace Mission Movement was organized into self-supporting communities which provided jobs, food, and housing. The movement ran its own businesses, including hotels and grocery stores. It also held Kingdom Banquets at which any hungry person was welcome.

Father Divine—who was also known as "Daddy Grace"—

One of Father Divine's peace missions in Harlem, New York City.
(Library of Congress)

forbade his followers to smoke, drink, use drugs, or gamble. He also demanded that his followers practice celibacy—refraining from sex. This meant no children were born and raised as followers. The number of Father Divine's followers at the height of the movement, in the mid-1930s, isn't known. They might have numbered as many as 2 million or as few as 50,000. Father Divine died in 1965, by which time the International Peace Mission Movement's membership had dwindled to a handful of followers.

Another new religious movement of the era—and one that was wholly African American—was the Nation of Islam. The movement's founder, W. D. Fard, was, like Father Divine, a somewhat mysterious figure. In 1930 Fard founded the Temple of Islam No. 1 in Detroit. Fard claimed that Islam was the "true religion of the black man," although his version of Islam was different in many important ways from traditional Islam. In 1934, Fard left Detroit and apparently disappeared. Leadership of the Nation of Islam passed to Elijah Poole, who took the name Elijah Muhammad.

Elijah Muhammad taught that African Americans should not seek equality with whites. Instead, he believed in the separation of the races and called for an African American "territory" within the United States. He also taught that African Americans had to become economically independent, so that they would not have to be involved in white society. Only then, he preached, would African Americans be able to reclaim the African identity they had lost through slavery in the United States. He also promoted the values of hard work and self-discipline among Nation of Islam members.

Under Elijah Mohammad's strict one-man leadership, the Nation of Islam won a small but highly motivated following in African American neighborhoods in northern cities, and in prisons. (Members of the Nation of Islam came to be known as Black Muslims, although they never used that name themselves.)

It wasn't until the 1960s—when the brilliant activist Malcolm X rose to a leadership role in the movement—that many Americans became aware of the Nation of Islam. In 1964, however, Malcolm X broke with the Nation of Islam and embraced the traditional Islam set forth in the Qu'aran.

When Elijah Muhammad died in 1975, the Nation of Islam split in two. One group, led by Elijah Muhammad's son, Warith Deen Muhammad, changed the movement's teachings to reflect traditional Islam. This group is now known as the American Muslim Mission. The other group, led by Louis Farrakhan, kept the Nation of Islam name and the original teachings of W. D. Fard and Elijah Muhammad.

Religion in the Depression

The Great Depression challenged churches and synagogues, as it did all aspects of American society. Most religious organizations tried to help those in need, often not only their own members but suffering people of all faiths (or none) in their communities.

As the Depression worsened, however, religious charities were stretched to the limit, and beyond. Many religious leaders began to call for the government to do more to help those people hurt by the Depression.

Some religious leaders were firm supporters of the New Deal. Others went even further and called for some form of socialist government. One Protestant minister in Chicago preached a sermon in which he stated, "No honest preacher, priest, or rabbi can dodge the square-cut issue. Something must be done right now toward remaking the sorely pressed world."

This was not a new idea. In the early 1900s, a Protestant

movement called the Social Gospel tried to combine Christianity with elements of socialism. That movement declined because of opposition from Fundamentalists. In the 1930s, however, the ideas of the Social Gospel got a new hearing.

The fear, uncertainty, and suffering of the Depression led some Americans to leave behind religious faith altogether in favor of radical political movements, especially communism. These people felt that a system like communism was the only way to save society from total collapse, and to make sure that peoples' basic needs were met. Communism, in fact, had elements that made it much like a form of religion.

But there were others who combined a commitment to social justice with religious faith. Among them was Dorothy Day, a young writer who was active in the Communist Party in the 1920s. In 1927, Day became a Roman Catholic. Many of her oldest friends turned their backs on her, because communism rejected all religions—especially Catholicism.

Dorothy Day
(Library of Congress)

Living in New York City during the worst years of the Depression, Day's faith found expression through her work with those hardest hit by the slump. In 1933, Day and Peter Maurin began to set up "Houses of Hospitality" to provide food for the hungry and shelter for the homeless. The two also began a newspaper, *The Catholic Worker*, to spread the word about their "radical Christian idealism." *The Catholic Worker* movement eventually influenced the leadership of the Catholic Church in America and inspired people of many faiths.

Day's selfless devotion to the poor lasted the rest of her life and led many to later call her a modern saint. It was a label she rejected. In her words, "We have lived with the poor, with the workers ... the unemployed, the sick .... We have learned that the only solution is love and that love comes with community."

Chapter Seven

Health, Science, and Technology

A public health campaign poster (LEFT) **produced by the City of Chicago Municipal Tuberculosis Sanitarium; Washington, DC citizens** (RIGHT) **wait for check-ups at a public health clinic.** (Library of Congress)

Much of the science and technology that marked the twentieth century took root in the United States in the 1920s and 1930s. During these twenty years, Americans came to accept many modern ideas about the physical and social world. They also began to communicate and travel in ways that were distinctly modern. And, thanks to modern medicine, they were living longer and healthier lives.

The ideas of Europeans such as Albert Einstein and Sigmund Freud found an audience in the United States. But American scientists, too, were beginning to publish new research in the social sciences about how people lived. Others made great strides in electronics and aviation technology. This was the age of radio, but television was developing. After some floundering, it also became an age of transcontinental and transoceanic flight. The seeds of space travel were also sown.

The fascist ideas that gave rise to the Holocaust in which 6 million Jews would perish brought many of Europe's scientists to American shores. With them came the knowledge that would help the United States build the first atomic bomb and become the world's most scientifically advanced nation.

A New View of the Universe

At the start of the 1920s, the big news in the world of science was Albert Einstein's Theory of Relativity. Einstein, a German-born physicist living in Switzerland, first proposed the theory in 1905 and expanded on it in 1916, but it didn't become widely known in America until after experiments in 1919 proved much of the theory.

In the very simplest terms, relativity stated that time and space were not fixed and unchanging. This overturned a view of the universe and its workings that had been commonly accepted for hundreds of years. Few people fully understood the complicated science behind relativity, but the basic idea fascinated many.

Einstein's work seemed to suggest that science-fiction concepts like travel through time were possible, at least in theory. Also, the excitement over relativity fueled the idea that the world had entered into a new era of scientific progress, in which science would solve all problems. Einstein himself became a huge celebrity. In 1933, after the Nazis came to power in Germany, Einstein came to the United States, settling at Princeton University in New Jersey.

The Social Sciences

Americans in the 1920s and 1930s were also fascinated by new ideas in the social sciences—those sciences that deal with humans and how they act as individuals and in groups.

In the field of psychiatry, the work of Austrian doctor Sigmund Freud was especially popular among writers, intellectuals, and other Modernist Americans. As with Einstein's Theory of Relativity, Freud's ideas were not new, but they weren't well known in America until the 1920s.

Just as Einstein overturned long-held views of the workings of the universe, Freud suggested a new way of looking at the workings of the mind. (Unlike Einstein's theories, however, Freud's ideas could not be scientifically proven.) In books like *On the Interpretation of Dreams*, Freud argued that human behavior had its roots in the "subconscious." He developed the new technique of "psychoanalysis," which he and his supporters claimed could help people overcome their mental problems.

Many traditionally minded Americans attacked Freud as a promoter of "immorality" because of his ideas about sex. His writings were a special target of Fundamentalists (see Chapter 6).

Nevertheless, many of the concepts he introduced worked their way into American life over the next few decades.

Another famous—and controversial—social scientist of the time was anthropologist Margaret Mead. (An anthropologist is a scientist who studies simple, non-literate cultures, usually in remote places.) In the 1920s Mead spent several years studying the people of the South Pacific islands of Samoa. She published her findings in 1928 in a book, *Coming of Age in Samoa*, which became a popular bestseller as well as an influential anthropological study.

In *Coming of Age in Samoa*, Mead suggested that the so-called "primitive people" of Samoa were actually happier than people in advanced, industrialized societies like America, because of the more easygoing way in which Samoan children were raised. In later books, she also challenged accepted ideas about the roles played by men and women in different societies. Although other anthropologists later questioned both her methods and her findings, Mead's ideas, like Freud's, became very influential.

In sociology, the study of group behavior, the husband and wife team of Robert and Helen Lynd helped Americans better understand the society they lived in through the Middletown studies. Starting in 1924, the Lynds surveyed the residents of Muncie, Indiana, about all aspects of their lives, from their religious beliefs to the kinds of appliances they had in their homes. The Lynds chose Muncie because they considered it the city most representative of America as a whole—"a typical city, strictly speaking, does not exist," they later wrote, "but the city studied was selected as having many features common to a wide group of communities."

In 1929, the Lynds published the results of their research in *Middletown: A Study in American Culture*. They returned to Muncie in the 1930s to see how the Depression had affected the city. The result was *Middletown in Transition*, published in 1937. The Lynd's work was a landmark exploration of how Americans lived their lives day by day in the 1920s and 1930s.

Health and Medicine

In general, Americans of the 1920s and 1930s lived longer and healthier lives than their parents and grandparents. This was partly due to better diet. Around the time of World War I, people became aware of the role that vitamins and nutrients play in maintaining health, and the importance of eating a variety of foods. As a result, people began to eat more fresh fruits, vegetables, and dairy products.

Among poorer Americans—especially those in the rural South—malnutrition was a problem, even in the prosperous 1920s. (Malnutrition is the condition of poor health that results when people don't have enough to eat, or don't eat enough of foods needed to stay healthy.) Malnutrition became a problem in many communities during the Depression.

The biggest single advance in medicine during the 1920s and 1930s was in the treatment and prevention of contagious diseases (those diseases that can be passed from person to person). Diseases like cholera, diphtheria, typhoid fever, and tuberculosis were still widespread in America in the early 20th century. In 1918 an epidemic of Spanish influenza, a respiratory disease, killed hundreds of thousands of Americans.

By the 1920s, however, doctors and public-health officials finally understood how germs spread disease. Along with better plumbing and sanitation, the use of disinfectants led to a big drop in the number of Americans dying of contagious diseases. Some diseases, like cholera, were practically eliminated.

A poster from the Chicago Board of Health warns about the danger of diphtheria.
(Library of Congress)

One disease that stubbornly resisted all attempts at prevention was poliomyelitis, or polio. Caused by a virus, this disease affected mainly children, leaving thousands dead or paralyzed every year in the 1920s and 1930s. The nation's most famous polio sufferer was President Franklin Roosevelt, who contracted the disease in 1921 as an adult. In the mid-1930s Roosevelt lent his name to a major fundraising campaign, the "March of Dimes," to support research into the dreaded disease. Unfortunately, it wasn't until the 1950s that scientists developed an effective vaccine to prevent the disease from developing in people.

Despite the overall improvement in health and advances in medicine, many Americans still had only limited access to medical care. Although the number of doctors in the United States rose during the

Future president Franklin D. Roosevelt, shortly before he was stricken with polio. (Library of Congress)

1930s and 1940s, their numbers didn't keep pace with the growing population. Also, most doctors practiced in towns and cities, leaving rural areas poorly served.

Many Americans of the era saw a doctor or entered a hospital only for emergencies or very serious conditions, because of the expense involved. In the 1920s some businesses offered their workers health insurance, which paid all or part of medical expenses for an employee and his or her family, but the number of people with medical insurance fell during the Depression. In 1940, less than 1 percent of the population was covered by any form of medical insurance. During the New Deal (see Overview) some politicians proposed a system of national medical insurance funded by the federal government, but there was much opposition from doctors, and the proposal was dropped.

Finally, one big change in health care in this era was the rise in hospital births. Before 1920, most American women gave birth at home, usually with the help of a doctor or midwife (a nurse trained to assist with childbirth). By 1940, however, more than half of all births in the United States took place in a hospital. This trend helped reduce the number of babies dying at birth or soon afterward by about half between 1920 and 1940.

Sound and Sight

The technological advance that had the most impact on Americans' daily lives in the 1920s was the development of radio technology.

In the late nineteenth century, Irish-Italian inventor Guglielmo Marconi proved that signals could be sent through the air. Early "wireless" sets, however, could only send and receive Morse code (dots and dashes representing letters). In 1906, Canadian-born engineer Reginald Fessenden introduced the alternator, the first high-frequency radio transmitter. Radio could now broadcast music and speech. In 1913, American engineer Lee DeForest developed an improved form of vacuum tube, the triode or "audion," which greatly amplified (strengthened) electrical currents. The triode was first used to improve long-distance telephone service before it was put to use in radios.

In 1920, the first radio station to make regular broadcasts, Pittsburgh's KDKA, reported the results of the presidential election. By the end of the decade, there were more than 600 radio

Having set her book aside, a young woman switches on a brand new radio, during the late 1920s. (Library of Congress)

stations across the country, and by 1933 more than two-thirds of American households had at least one radio.

In most American homes, the radio became the "electronic hearth" around which the family gathered for news and entertainment. During the Great Depression, observers noted that some jobless people would rather sell off their furniture before parting with their radio.

The 1920s and 1930s also saw the start of a technology that would one day have an even greater impact on American life than radio—television.

Like many important inventions, television developed over decades, in different countries, and several people contributed to its development. By the mid-1920s, inventors had shown that images could be transmitted over the airwaves.

The first television broadcast in the United States came in 1927, when a small group of telephone-company executives in New York City watched and heard Secretary of Commerce (and future president) Herbert Hoover speak from his office in Washington, D.C. These early televisions, however, used a combination of mechanical and electronic technology and their image quality was poor.

In the early 1920s, a Russian-born American scientist, Vladimir Zworykin, developed a fully electronic television system. During this same period, Philo T. Farnsworth, another American inventor, developed a very similar system. Although the U.S. Patent Office later ruled that Farnsworth was the "inventor" of television in the United States, Zworykin's claim was championed by David Sarnoff, head of the powerful Radio Corporation of America (RCA), the company that took the early lead in developing television for commercial purposes.

A few mostly experimental TV stations began broadcasting in the 1930s, but it wasn't until 1939 that most Americans became aware of the possibilities of television, when RCA held demonstrations of the new technology at the World's Fair in New York City. By the end of 1940, about 5,000 U.S. households had TV sets.

When the United States entered World War II in 1941, the government ordered a halt in the manufacture of televisions because their electronic components were needed for the war effort. It would take another decade before TVs replaced radios as the "electronic hearth" of the American home.

America Takes Wing

Sound and pictures weren't the only things traveling through the air in the 1920s and 1930s. For the first time, people took to the skies in large numbers.

In 1920, the airplane was only seventeen years old. Most Americans had never even seen a plane, let alone flown in one. The next twenty years, however, were a time of amazing advances in aviation. By 1940, airplanes were a common sight in America's skies, and Americans could cross the continent in less than a day and cross the oceans in a matter of days.

World War I (1914–1918) gave a boost to the new science of aviation. All the countries involved in the war used aircraft to scout enemy positions, drop bombs, and fight enemy planes. A new kind of hero, the fighter pilot, came on the scene. Americans thrilled to stories of "ace" fighter pilots, like America's own Captain Eddie Rickenbacker, dueling in the skies over Europe.

When the war ended, however, public interest in flying dropped off. Despite the progress in aviation during the war, aircraft at the start of the 1920s were still crude machines. They could fly only relatively short distances, and even the largest

World War I flying ace
Eddie Rickenbacker
(National Archives)

planes could carry only a few passengers. Engines often failed. Crashes were commonplace. To many Americans, it seemed like it would be a long time before airplanes became practical, reliable vehicles for carrying passengers.

Some farsighted pilots and aviation enthusiasts believed otherwise, and they did all they could to promote commercial aviation. Many of them were former military pilots. During the war, the U.S. Army had trained thousands of pilots and ordered thousands of planes, but the war had ended before either pilots or planes could get into action. Most pilots returned to civilian life; others were determined to keep flying, one way or another.

For those who wanted to fly, there were plenty of war-surplus planes around at the start of the 1920s. The most common wartime model, the Curtiss JN-4, or "Jenny," a two-seater biplane (a plane with two wings) sold for just $300, not much more than a Model T Ford. Hundreds of ex-military pilots (and others with a taste for aerial adventure) bought these surplus planes and began "barnstorming" around the country.

Many Americans got their first glimpse of a plane when a barnstormer appeared over their town or farm, looping-the-loop or performing other daring "aerobatics" to attract attention before landing in a field or local fairground. Then the pilot would offer to take anyone for a ride for, say, $5. (If an interested local

"Fearless Freddie," a Hollywood stunt man, clinging to a rope ladder slung from a plane, about to drop into an automobile below. (Library of Congress)

asked what would happen if they crashed, the barnstormer's usual reply was "You'll get your money back.")

Soon individual barnstormers joined together into "flying circuses" that traveled the countryside giving exhibitions for money at county fairs and other events. These daredevil pilots developed a wide variety of stunts to entertain the local people. There was "wing-walking," for example, in which one pilot strode around on the wing or even hung off the landing gear while another flew the plane. (Wing-walking was less dangerous than it looked; most wing-walkers used thin wires, invisible from the ground, to secure themselves to the plane.) Other stunts included parachute jumps, aerobatics, and mock "dogfights" (serial combat between planes). The fact that stunts sometimes went wrong, leading to crashes, only seemed to add to the crowd's excitement.

Barnstorming and stunt flying, however, were hard, risky ways to make a living, and they didn't pay very well. Also, flying as entertainment didn't do much to advance the cause of aviation as an industry.

Carrying the Mail

If the planes of the early 1920s were generally too small and dangerous for regular passenger service, they could at least carry mail. In fact, the U.S. Postal Service began airmail service in 1918, using army pilots, but only between a few cities on the East Coast.

In 1921 the Postal Service decided to experiment with coast-to-coast airmail service. The first test flight didn't have encouraging results. Of the four planes involved, one crashed (killing the pilot), one was grounded by bad weather, one got lost, and only one got through with its load of mail—barely.

The problem was that for planes to carry mail faster than trains, they had to be able to fly at night. Unfortunately, in those days before radar and other navigational aids, it was hard for pilots to find their way in the dark, when they couldn't use things on the ground—like rivers and railroad tracks—as guides.

The solution, which saved the airmail program, was to set up powerful electric beacons (searchlights pointed skyward) at regular spaces along each airmail route. In 1924 airmail flights began on the first such lighted "airway" between Chicago, Illinois, and Cheyenne, Wyoming. Eventually 18,000 miles of lighted airways crisscrossed the continent. By 1925, an airmail letter from New York could reach San Francisco in about thirty hours; regular mail took three days.

In 1925, Congress passed a law called the Kelly Act, which called on the Postal Service to use private companies, with their own pilots, to fly the mail. The Kelly Act had a huge effect on the future of American aviation. Several of the companies that won post office contracts in the mid- and late 1920s soon began carrying passengers as well. Some major airlines, including American Airlines, Transcontinental Air Transport (TAT, which became TWA), and Pan-American got their start as mail carriers under the Kelly Act.

Airmail was now a part of daily life, but flying the mail had its dangers. Because they had to keep to a schedule, airmail pilots flew in all but the very worst weather. Crashes remained frequent. Often, pilots caught in storms at night took their chances with a parachute rather than attempt a landing in the dark on unknown ground. In late 1926, one young airmail pilot was the subject of a few small news stories when he was forced to "bail out" twice in a single six-week period. His name was Charles A. Lindbergh.

Going the Distance

Meanwhile, daring pilots continued to prove that long-distance flying was at least possible, even if it wasn't yet practical for regular passenger service. In May 1923, two army pilots made the first nonstop coast-to-coast flight, from New York to California in twenty-seven hours. A year later, four army planes took off from Seattle in an attempt to fly around the world. Two were lost in crashes but two made it back to Seattle five months later.

Flying the Atlantic, which separated America from Europe, was what really captured the public's attention in the mid-1920s. The Atlantic had actually crossed several times since 1919 both by land-based planes and seaplanes (planes that can land and take off on water) as well as by airships (large aircraft that use helium or hydrogen, gases which are lighter than air, to stay aloft).

When a French-born American businessman named Raymond Orteig offered a $25,000 prize to the first pilot to make a nonstop flight between New York and Paris, public interest in transatlantic flight picked up: now it was a race. It would be a costly race. In 1926 and early 1927 there were four attempts—two by French airmen, two by Americans—to claim the prize. All failed, with the loss, altogether, of six pilots and crew.

Then, in the spring of 1927, Charles Lindbergh announced he was going for the prize. Most thought he didn't have a chance. Instead of flying a multi-engined plane with at least a co-pilot, Lindbergh proposed going it alone, in a small single-engined plane, the *Spirit of St. Louis*. (A group of St. Louis businessmen sponsored Lindbergh's attempt.)

On the rainy morning of May 20, Lindbergh took off from Roosevelt Field, Long Island, New York, barely clearing the telephone wires at the end of the runway. Without a radio, he was out of contact with the world, which waited breathlessly for news. Thirty-three and a half hours later, he touched down at Le Bourget airport outside Paris.

America—and the world—went wild with celebration. Overnight, the 25 year-old pilot became the most famous person alive. The amazing response to "Lindy's" feat gave aviation the big boost it needed to win public acceptance.

Passenger Aviation

After Lindbergh's flight, U.S. domestic aviation (passenger travel between points within the country), which had lagged behind that of Europe, finally started to develop.

Henry Ford grasped the airplane's importance in the early 1920s, just as he had realized the automobile's potential decades before. In 1924, Ford's engineers began work on a plane that Ford hoped would be the Model T of the air. The result was the Ford 4-AT, which first flew in 1926, and an improved version, the 5-AT, followed in 1928.

The Ford Tri-Motor, as it was called from its three engines, did share some qualities with the Model T. The "tin goose" was not very graceful or fast, but it was rugged, reliable, and easy to maintain, and it could carry fifteen passengers at a top speed of about 110 miles per hour.

Also like the Model T, the Tri-Motor wasn't particularly comfortable for its passengers. Vibration and engine noise made conversation practically impossible during flight. The plane could only fly at a relatively low altitude (height), where the air is often "bumpy" with turbulence. That made flight in a Ford Tri-Motor often bone-shaking and stomach-churning.

Still, the Ford Tri-Motor was a big advance in passenger air-

The Lone Eagle

Charles Lindbergh's 1927 flight made him the greatest celebrity of the 1920s. He remained in the public eye throughout the 1930s, too, though for very different reasons. In a way, Lindbergh's life reflected the life of America as a nation—triumph in the 1920s, tragedy in the 1930s.

Charles Augustus Lindbergh was born in 1902. The son of a U.S. congressman, he grew up in Washington, D.C., and Minnesota, fascinated by flight. He was a barnstormer, U.S. Army Air Service pilot, and airmail pilot before he flew into history.

Lindbergh seemed an ideal hero. He was quiet, modest, and didn't smoke or drink. In a decade when newspapers were filled with sensational stories about flamboyant movie stars, corrupt politicians, and gangsters, the young flier seemed to represent the "old American" qualities of hard work, self-reliance, and pioneer spirit.

After returning to the U.S., Lindbergh made several "goodwill flights" at the request of the government. On one, he met Anne Morrow, daughter of the U.S. ambassador to Mexico, whom he married.

In March 1932, the Lindberghs' 20-month-old son, Charles Lindbergh, Jr., was kidnapped from the family home in Hopewell, New Jersey. Two months later the baby's body was found nearby.

A German-born carpenter, Bruno Hauptmann, was later arrested for the crime. His trial ranks with the Scopes Trial (see page 88) as one of the most famous—and controversial—of the era. Although some evidence connected Hauptmann to the crime, there was no real proof he had caused the baby's death. Nevertheless, he was convicted and executed in 1936. Heartbroken and overwhelmed by the ordeal of the trial, the Lindberghs moved to England.

When war broke out in Europe, the Lindberghs returned to America. Always uncomfortable with fame, Lindbergh used it in the service of a cause he believed in—keeping America out of World War II. He joined the America First Committee and became the Isolationist movement's most famous spokesperson.

In a September 1941 speech, Lindbergh criticized American Jews for favoring intervention in the war. This speech, and the fact that Lindbergh had accepted awards from Nazi Germany, led many Americans to attack him as a pro-Nazi anti-Semite. Once America's greatest hero, he now appeared to have become almost a traitor.

When the U.S. entered the war, Lindbergh volunteered for combat but was turned away. Instead, he served as a consultant to the U.S. Army Air Force in the Pacific. After the war, Lindbergh's reputation recovered. In his last years he became a strong supporter of environmentalism.

(Library of Congress)

craft. It was the plane of choice for most early U.S. airlines, including Transcontinental Air Transport (TAT), which began the first regular coast-to-coast passenger service in July 1929. (The airline called itself the "Lindbergh Line" because it employed Charles Lindbergh as a consultant.)

Because it was still too dangerous to carry passengers at night, TAT's service combined planes with trains: Passengers would fly during the day, board a train for an overnight leg of the journey, then resume flying in the morning. The trip between New York and Los Angeles took two days, only one day less than the train. For most people, the inconvenience (and high ticket price) wasn't justified by the savings in time. The coast-to-coast service was canceled in 1930.

As it had with airmail, technology came to the rescue. In this case, it was the development of radio navigation that revived long-distance passenger service. Powerful radio transmitters were set up to "beam" signals which pilots could follow, even at night or in bad weather.

Radio also allowed communication with the ground, which led to the development of the air-traffic-control system. Early airports were often just open fields with a shed to shelter arriving and departing passengers. They gave way to sophisticated terminals capable of handling several planes at once.

Even the coming of the Depression didn't slow the growth of domestic aviation. By the end of the 1930s, U.S. airlines were carrying 3 million passengers each year. However, only a small percentage of the population flew regularly. Flying remained a relatively expensive way to travel. Most passengers were business-people or others for whom time was money. Still, the growth of domestic aviation from 1928 to 1940 was amazing, considering that the number of passengers carried before then was in the thousands.

Flying became much safer, faster, and more comfortable in the 1930s, too. In 1930 Boeing Air Transport (BAT), which later became United Airlines, hired eight young women to serve as "stewardesses" on its San Francisco-Chicago flights. (The women were all trained nurses, and they wore nurse's uniforms. BAT's management thought their presence would calm nervous passengers.) Other airlines followed suit. These early "air hostesses" served meals (almost always chicken salad and coffee) and generally tried to keep passengers comfortable.

Faster, more sophisticated passenger planes began to replace the slow, shaky Ford Tri-Motor. In the early years the Ford Tri-Motor had some competition from another three-engined plane, the Fokker F-10, which was a European design. In 1931, however, the U.S. government grounded all Fokkers after a crash which killed eight people, including Knute Rockne, the famous Notre Dame football coach.

That same year, BAT introduced a remarkable aircraft, the Model 247. (In the early 1930s the airline built its own planes, but in 1934 the federal government ruled that Boeing's passenger-carrying and aircraft-manufacturing operations had to be separated.) The two-engined 247 could carry ten passengers, less than the Ford Tri-Motor, but it could fly much faster and was much more comfortable, thanks to a soundproofed cabin.

To meet the competition from Boeing, Trans-World Airlines (TWA, TAT's successor) turned to the Douglas Company to design and build an even better plane. The result was the DC-2, which first flew in 1933 and cut the coast-to-coast flying time to twenty hours.

In 1935 Douglas introduced the DC-3, which became perhaps the most successful airplane in history. More than 10,000 DC-3s were built and some were still flying in the 21st century. By the end of the 1930s, nine out of every ten U.S. passenger planes were DC-2s or DC-3s.

The Douglas Company's DC-3 helped popularize airplane travel. (Library of Congress)

Space and the Atom

In the 1920s, one American scientist conducted experiments that were little noticed at the time, but which would later help Americans set foot on the moon and explore outer space.

Robert Goddard was a professor at Clark University in Massachusetts. Around the time of World War I, Goddard began experimenting with liquid-fuel rockets. At first Goddard intended his rockets to carry instruments to study the earth's upper atmosphere. Goddard, however, came to believe that powerful rockets could break free of the earth's atmosphere altogether, and travel into space.

In 1920, Goddard published two scientific papers "A Method of Reaching Extreme Altitudes" and "Report on Further Developments of the Rocket Method of Investigating Space." The papers brought a brief period of public interest in Goddard's work. A *New York Times* headline declared, "AIM TO REACH MOON WITH NEW ROCKET."

When it became clear that Goddard's work was still very experimental, the public lost interest. One of Goddard's biggest problems was finding the money to continue his experiments. Later, Lindbergh convinced some wealthy associates to help support Goddard's efforts. On March 16, 1926, Goddard launched a rocket that flew 2.5 seconds and traveled 184 feet. While this didn't seem like an impressive performance, it proved that a liquid-fuel engine could power a rocket.

Robert Goddard
(Library of Congress)

Goddard moved his experiments from Massachusetts to New Mexico to work on the next challenge—a "guidance system" to keep the rocket stable in flight. In the 1930s, Goddard launched rockets that reached heights of 9,000 feet and flew faster than the speed of sound. Goddard died in 1945, at the dawn of the "Space Age" he had pioneered.

In the late 1930s, other scientists explored the space inside the atom.

One side-effect of the rise of dictators in Europe was that some of the greatest scientists in the world fled to the United States, including Germany's Einstein, Leo Szilard and Edward Teller of Hungary, Niels Bohr of Denmark, and Enrico Fermi of Italy. Together with native-born scientists like Ernest Lawrence and J. Robert Oppenheimer, these brilliant refugees would make the United States the world's most scientifically advanced nation.

At the time, however, the refugee scientists had a pressing concern. Part of Einstein's work on relativity suggested that the massive amounts of energy within the atom could be released through a process called fission. This meant that a devastating new weapon—an atomic bomb—was possible.

The refugee scientists knew that scientists in Germany were working on atomic fission, and they feared what would happen if a brutal dictatorship like the Nazi regime developed atomic weapons. In the summer of 1939, several scientists asked Einstein to write a letter to President Franklin Roosevelt warning of the danger and urging government support for American atomic experiments.

This letter led to the creation of the Office of Scientific Research and Development and, ultimately, the Manhattan Project, the program that created the first atomic bombs. The atomic bombing of Japan in August 1945 ended World War II, but it also unleashed a new and terrible force in the world. Einstein later said that writing the letter to President Roosevelt was the greatest mistake of his life.

Albert Einstein
Old Grove Rd.
Nassau Point
Peconic, Long Island

August 2nd, 1939

F.D. Roosevelt,
President of the United States,
White House
Washington, D.C.

Sir:

Some recent work by E.Fermi and L. Szilard, which has been communicated to me in manuscript, leads me to expect that the element uranium may be turned into a new and important source of energy in the immediate future. Certain aspects of the situation which has arisen seem to call for watchfulness and, if necessary, quick action on the part of the Administration. I believe therefore that it is my duty to bring to your attention the following facts and recommendations:

In the course of the last four months it has been made probable - through the work of Joliot in France as well as Fermi and Szilard in America - that it may become possible to set up a nuclear chain reaction in a large mass of uranium, by which vast amounts of power and large quantities of new radium-like elements would be generated. Now it appears almost certain that this could be achieved in the immediate future.

This new phenomenon would also lead to the construction of bombs, and it is conceivable - though much less certain - that extremely powerful bombs of a new type may thus be constructed. A single bomb of this type, carried by boat and exploded in a port, might very well destroy the whole port together with some of the surrounding territory. However, such bombs might very well prove to be too heavy for transportation by air.

Albert Einstein wrote this letter to President Roosevelt to warn him about German efforts to make an atom bomb.
(National Archives)

Chapter Eight

Leisure, Sports, and Entertainment

Tennis star Helen Wills (LEFT); the original "Hollywoodland" sign in the hills over Hollywood. (RIGHT) Although the famous sign still stands today, it now only reads "Hollywood." (Library of Congress)

In the 1920s many Americans had money in their pockets and plenty of free time—often for the first time in their lives. Millions of people spent their newfound income and leisure hours at the ballpark, the movie theater, or dancing to the new sounds of jazz. These decades were also a time of great creativity in the "lively arts," like theater and journalism.

The Depression stalled, but didn't stop, the nation's pursuit of pleasure. The movies took people's minds off the hard times, while the radio brought entertainment right into America's homes.

Some historians have called the 1920s and 1930s the golden age of sports in America. Attendance at ballparks and football stadiums reached heights never seen before, while radio made it possible for Americans to follow games in their homes. The top athletes became huge celebrities, second only to movie stars in their popularity with the people. America's most popular spectator sport was baseball.

Play Ball!

Baseball started the era at a low point. In 1919, members of the Chicago White Sox were found to have "thrown" the World

Babe Ruth

Babe Ruth was the greatest American sports star of the 1920s and probably the greatest celebrity of the era after Charles Lindbergh. In many ways, Babe Ruth is a perfect symbol for America in the 1920s. He was among the most colorful, larger-than-life personalities in a decade filled with flamboyant figures.

Born in Baltimore in 1895, George Herman Ruth grew up in poverty. He first played pro ball for the Baltimore Orioles (then a minor-league team) in 1914, where he got his famous nickname. After a few months the short, stocky southpaw moved up to the Boston Red Sox.

In 1920 the Red Sox sold Ruth's contract to the New York Yankees. Over the next couple of seasons the hitter rose to fame as the "Sultan of Swat." In the words of one sportswriter of the era, "After the Black Sox scandal, Babe Ruth with his bat pounded baseball back into popularity."

Ruth led the team to seven pennants and four World Series victories between 1920 and 1933. In his best year, 1927, he hit sixty home runs—a single-season record that would stand for thirty-four years. His lifetime record of 714 home runs remained unbroken until Hank Aaron hit his 715th homer in 1974.

By 1930 Ruth's salary was $80,000, a huge sum for the time. When a reporter told him that was $5,000 more than President Herbert Hoover was paid, Ruth replied, "I know, but I had a better year."

The statistics only tell part of the story. Ruth was famous not just for his achievements on the field, but for his antics off it. Ruth was a man with big appetites for alcohol, food, and wild behavior. "He was a circus, a play and a movie, all rolled into one," in the words of his teammate Lefty Gomez. Mindful of his own hard childhood, Ruth was also famous for his kindness to children.

Ruth left the Yankees after the 1934 season. After a short stint as manager for the Boston Braves in 1935, he retired from baseball. The following year he was among the first players elected to the National Baseball Hall of Fame. He spent his retirement pursuing his passion for golf. In June 1948, suffering from cancer, he made one last emotional appearance at Yankee Stadium, "the house that Ruth built." Two months later he was dead.

(Library of Congress)

Series—losing on purpose to help professional gamblers. The so-called "Black Sox" Scandal was a severe blow to the national pastime. Baseball recovered, though, after the owners of the nation's 16 major-league teams agreed to the appointment of a commissioner to oversee professional ball. The first commissioner was Kenesaw Mountain Landis, a former federal judge.

The great stars of the era were the home-run hitters, like Lou Gehrig and Joe DiMaggio of the New York Yankees and Jimmie Foxx of the Philadelphia Athletics, and the greatest of them all was the Yankees' Babe Ruth (see page 115). The Yankees dominated the game during the 1920s and 1930s. They won a total of eight World Series championships between 1920 and 1940, including four straight series from 1936 through 1939.

African American ballplayers couldn't play in the major leagues at this time, but the flourishing Negro Leagues included some of the best players of the day. They included Josh Gibson, Leroy "Satchel" Paige, and James "Cool Papa" Bell. Gibson was such a powerful hitter he became known as "the black Babe Ruth." Sportswriters who saw both men play suggested that Babe Ruth should be called "the white Josh Gibson."

Lou Gehrig
(Library of Congress)

On the Gridiron

College football was actually the biggest sport of the 1920s and 1930s, in terms of attendance at games. For millions of Americans, Saturday afternoon at a university's stadium became an autumn ritual.

Before the 1920s, teams from "Ivy League" schools and from the army and navy academies dominated college football. During the decade, however, two teams from midwestern universities won the admiration of football fans across the nation.

The first was the "Fighting Irish" of Notre Dame University in South Bend, Indiana. The key to Notre Dame's success on the gridiron was its brilliant coach, Knute Rockne. He had an amazing ability to both find great players and inspire them to do their best. Of the 105 games Notre Dame played between 1919 and 1931, they won all but twelve, with five ties.

The other team that rose to nationwide fame in the 1920s was the University of Illinois, thanks to halfback Red Grange, the "Galloping Ghost." A three-time All-American, Grange made touchdown runs totaling 262 yards in a single game against Michigan in 1924.

The following year, Grange signed a contract to play professional football with the Chicago Bears. At this time, professional football lagged behind baseball and college football in popularity. Grange's move to pro ball boosted public acceptance of the game. It also helped save the struggling National Football League (NFL), which had been founded in 1922. By the end of the 1930s, a million fans a year were attending pro football games.

Red Grange
(Library of Congress)

Golf and Tennis

The sports boom of the 1920s was not limited to "big league" sports. Golf and tennis grew in popularity both as spectator sports and as leisure-time activities.

Golf, especially, became a passion for many Americans in the 1920s. In earlier decades, golf was mainly a game for the wealthy. It required a lot of time to play, and it usually cost a lot to belong to a country club with a golf course. As Americans' work week shortened, more people had time to spend on the course. Many communities built public courses. By the end of the 1920s, there were more than 4,000 golf courses in the United States—up from around 1,000 in 1900. Three million people played golf regularly.

Bobby Jones
(Library of Congress)

As a spectator sport, golf's popularity got a boost from the career of Bobby Jones. An Atlanta lawyer, Jones was not a professional golfer, but he played in professional tournaments. From 1923 to 1930, Jones won thirteen of the twenty-one tournaments he entered, and in 1930 he astonished the world by winning all four of golf's greatest tournaments—the British Open, British Amateur, U.S. Open, and U.S. Amateur. Borrowing a term from the card game bridge, sportswriters dubbed Jones's feat the "Grand Slam." No golfer since has won all four tournaments in a single year.

Tennis, too, went from being mainly a country-club sport to an activity enjoyed by millions. The 1920s also saw tennis become a popular spectator sport, thanks largely to two players, William "Big Bill" Tilden and Helen Wills.

The two had very different styles. Tilden's dramatic way of play proved to many that tennis could be as exciting to watch as baseball or football. Wills, on the other hand, was nicknamed "Little Miss Poker Face" for her businesslike manner on the court. Both dominated the sport during the era. From 1920 to 1926, Tilden won six U.S. Championships (now known as the U.S. Open) in a row and won it again in 1929. Between 1923 and 1938 Wills won nineteen major U.S. and international tournaments and an Olympic gold medal. In 1935 the Associated Press named her Female Athlete of the Year.

Other Sports Stars

Jesse Owens
(Library of Congress)

Other famous athletes of the era include the swimmer Gertrude Ederle, who made headlines in 1926 when she became the first woman to swim the twenty-six-mile English Channel between England and France, beating the fastest men's time in the process.

One of the great American Olympic athletes was track-and-field star Jesse Owens, who won four gold medals and set three world records at the 1936 Olympics in Berlin, Germany. Owens's victories were especially sweet to many Americans because he was an African American. His stunning perform-ance made a mockery of Germany's Nazi regime, which held that racial and ethnic minorities were "inferior."

Jack Dempsey
(Library of Congress)

Heavyweight boxing was a popular sport during these years. In the 1920s, Jack Dempsey and Gene Tunney vied for the heavyweight crown. Their 1927 bout at Soldier Field in Chicago drew a crowd of more than 100,000. (Tunney won, thanks in part to a controversial call from a referee.)

Joe Louis
(Library of Congress)

Joe Louis, an African American fighter who turned pro in 1935, was famous for knocking out his opponents. That year, in the midst of the Depression, he won $350,000 and was named Male Athlete of the Year. In 1936, Louis lost his first professional fight to German Max Schmeling, a former heavyweight champ. But several wins later, in 1937, Louis captured the heavyweight title. In 1938, with Hitler touting Schmeling as an ideal of racial purity, Louis defeated him. Like Owens's Olympic triumph, the Louis-Schmelling rematch was seen by many as a victory not just for African Americans, but for all Americans. Louis defended the heavyweight title a record twenty-five times and retired in 1946.

Music, Music, Music

The 1920s and 1930s saw a variety of musical styles—jazz and blues, country, and the "big band" sound—become part of American popular culture. The rise of radio did much to give Americans a "soundtrack" to their daily lives. So did records, which finally gave people a way to listen to the music they wanted, when they wanted—although the records of the day could only hold about five minutes of music on each side.

Sales of most kinds of records dropped in the mid-1920s because of competition from radio, but they picked up in the mid-1930s when coin-operated jukeboxes began to appear in bars, restaurants, and other public places. The jukebox let people choose from a selection of records at five cents per play. By the end of the 1930s, more than half of all records produced in the United States went into jukeboxes.

Jazz and Blues

The 1920s is sometimes called the Jazz Age because the decade saw this uniquely American form of music achieve widespread popularity. Jazz developed around the turn of the 20th century in African American neighborhoods in New Orleans. It evolved from a mix of influences, including African music brought to America by slaves, European band music, and earlier musical styles like ragtime.

What made jazz unique was improvisation. Instead of playing notes from a written score, jazz musicians took a tune and played variations on it. Different instruments—trumpet or cornet, trombone, clarinet—played solos in turn, while drums and sometimes a banjo kept up the rhythm.

As African Americans moved from the South to the cities of the North and Midwest, jazz traveled with them. By the early 1920s, jazz began to spread into the wider American society. Early jazz was dance music, and jazz provided the accompaniment for popular dances like the Charleston and the Turkey Trot.

Not everyone was a fan. Many traditionally minded Americans felt that jazz, with its hard-driving "syncopated" rhythms, was "corrupting the morals" of the nation's young people. The music's African American origins and the fact that it was often played in speakeasies (see Chapter 2), also made it a target. Others began to appreciate jazz as an inventive new musical

Joe "King" Oliver's jazz band featured a young cornet player named Louis Armstrong (THIRD FROM RIGHT). **Armstrong, who soon switched to trumpet, would become one of the most important musicians in American history.** (Library of Congress)

style. Broadway composer George Gershwin wrote a piece, "Rhapsody in Blue," that included elements of jazz in 1924.

As jazz grew in popularity, white musicians began to play it too. Some, like the great cornetist Bix Beiderbecke, played in the "hot" style of their African American counterparts. But others, like the bandleader Paul Whiteman, developed a smoother, blander version of jazz. By the early 1930s this watered-down version of jazz dominated the radio and record sales.

At the same time, however, two African American musicians did more than any others to raise jazz to an American art form. The first was Louis Armstrong. After growing up in great poverty in New Orleans, Armstrong took his trumpet to Chicago in 1922 and became a star player in Joe "King" Oliver's band. Over the next decade, Armstrong made a series of records with his band, the Hot Fives (later the Hot Sevens), which took jazz to a new level, thanks to his amazing solos.

The second was Duke Ellington, a pianist, bandleader, and composer. Born into a middle-class family in Washington, D.C., Ellington perfected an elegant style of jazz that brought white audiences "uptown" to the Cotton Club, the Harlem nightclub that hosted his orchestra in the 1920s. Ellington's music was the soundtrack to the Harlem Renaissance, a period of great creativity in literature, music, and the arts in New York City's African-American community. Ironically, the Cotton Club and other nightclubs were segregated—African Americans were welcome as performers, but not as audience members.

Another musical style that spread from South to North during the 1920s was the blues—songs of hardship and heartbreak rooted deeply in the African American experience. Because blues music was rarely played on the radio, it spread mostly through "race" records sold in African American neighborhoods. The greatest blues singer of the time was Bessie Smith, the "Empress of the Blues."

Country Music

Along with jazz and blues, country music—usually called hillbilly or mountain music—found its way onto records and the radio in the 1920s and 1930s.

Like jazz, country music developed over many years and from a variety of sources, including the ballads brought to America by settlers from England, Ireland, and Scotland. Also like jazz, country music spread as people moved from the South to the North and Midwest in search of jobs.

A big step in the establishment of country music came in October 1925 when radio station WSM in Nashville, Tennessee, began broadcasting a Saturday night country music show. First called the National Barn Dance, but better known as the Grand Ole Opry, the show launched the careers of many country performers.

Another major event in the history of country music came two years later, in 1927, when the Victor Record Company sent Ralph Peer to Bristol, Tennessee, to record local musicians. From these "Bristol sessions" came the first records from Jimmie Rodgers and the Carter family, two of the greatest and most influential of the early country performers.

Big Bands, Swing, and Crooners

In the mid-1930s, a new form of jazz—swing—got America dancing. Like early jazz out of New Orleans, swing featured up-tempo rhythms, improvisation, and instrumental solos. Swing bands, however, were larger than the early jazz bands, with a wider variety of instruments.

Although the "big bands" usually included singers, the band-leaders were the featured soloists and the real stars. Great band-leaders of the time included Count Basie (piano), Jimmy Dorsey (saxophone and clarinet), his brother Tommy (trombone), Glenn Miller (trombone), and Artie Shaw (clarinet). The leaders of the most popular bands were celebrities.

Swing was music for dancing, and swing fans—mostly young people—"cut the rug" with a variety of high-energy dance styles, like the jitterbug, the lindy hop, and the big apple. Swing even developed its own slang vocabulary. A fan who liked drummer Gene Krupa's style, for example, was a "hepcat" who was "knocked out" by Krupa's "skin-beating." (Drums of the era were topped with animal hide.)

"Hot" music was for energetic dancing; "sweet" tunes were more melodic, and usually featured a female singer. Some of the finest singers of the swing era were Martha Tilton (who sang with Benny Goodman's band), Billie Holiday (Artie Shaw's vocalist), and a trio, the Andrews Sisters.

Popular male vocalists were known as "crooners" for the way they sang closely and softly into the microphone. Bing Crosby was the most famous crooner, but by the end of the 1930s he had competition from a young singer named Frank Sinatra, who sang with Harry James and Tommy Dorsey.

Benny Goodman led one of the most popular swing bands in history. (Library of Congress)

Hollywood's Heyday

For most Americans of the 1920s and 1930s, the most popu-lar leisure-time activity was undoubtedly going to the movies. At the start of the 1920s about 35 million Americans went to the movies at least once a week, and that number more than doubled by the end of the decade.

The movies came to influence all aspects of American life, from fashions to the relationship between the sexes. It was dur-ing this era that the term Hollywood (from the section of Los Angeles where most major movie studios were located) came to mean the movies in the same way that Wall Street meant finance.

In an era of celebrities, movie stars were the biggest celebri-ties of all. Comedian Charlie Chaplin, the dashing Douglas Fairbanks, female "starlets" ranging from the wholesome Mary

Pickford to the saucy Clara Bow—all received huge salaries and were adored by armies of fans. The most eager moviegoers followed every detail of their favorite stars' lives, onscreen and off, in newspapers and in magazines like *Photoplay*.

Some fans worshipped their silver-screen heroes to the point of obsession. When Rudolph Valentino—famous as a romantic "leading man" in movies like 1921's *The Sheik*—died in 1926, 30,000 grieving fans mobbed the New York funeral home where his body lay.

As with jazz, the movies of the 1920s came under fire from conservative critics. With movies so popular, these critics believed that moviegoers would imitate the behavior they saw onscreen, from cigarette smoking to drinking. Religious leaders, especially, charged that scenes of sexual behavior and violence encouraged immorality and crime. Stars' behavior off-screen came in for criticism, too, after several scandals involving sex and drugs rocked Hollywood in the 1920s.

By the early 1930s some religious groups, especially the Roman Catholic Church, threatened to ban their members from going to the movies until Hollywood "cleaned up its act." Faced with the prospect of losing millions of moviegoers, Hollywood did so. In 1934, the major studios agreed to a "production code" which set out what could, and could not, be shown onscreen.

The Talkies

A technical advance of the 1920s—the coming of sound—helped make moviegoing even more popular. From the time motion pictures came to America around the turn of the 20th century, they were silent, and usually shown to the accompaniment of a piano or organ.

There were several early attempts at synchronizing (playing together) sound and film, but most of the major movie studios were not very interested. Movies seemed popular enough, and installing sound equipment in theaters would be expensive. (At this time, movie studios also owned most movie theaters.)

In 1926, however, Warner Brothers, one of the biggest studios, decided to adapt the Vitaphone process for sound films. The first full-length movie with sound, *The Jazz Singer*, opened in New York City the following year. Warner Brothers' gamble paid off. *The Jazz Singer* was a huge hit. The Vitaphone process was not perfect. A new system was developed, however, and the major studios soon adopted it. By 1930 half the nation's movie theaters were equipped to show "talkies," and practically all of them would be within a few years.

Hollywood in the 1930s

Despite the popularity of the talkies, Hollywood didn't escape the Depression. By 1933, ticket sales had fallen by about 25 percent from their 1930 level. Many theaters closed down, and movie studios were in serious financial trouble. Within a couple of years, however, Hollywood made an amazing recovery. Americans began going to the movies again in large numbers—85 million per week, on average. The movies became a cheap way to escape the cares and worries of hard times, for a few hours at least.

Moviegoers of the 1930s got a lot of entertainment for the price of a ticket—which was usually twenty or twenty-five cents, ten cents for children. A typical "Saturday matinee" would began with a newsreel—a short film depicting current events around the world.

Next was usually a serial. Aimed mainly at children, these were short films in which the action unfolded week by week. Each week's episode ended in a "cliffhanger," with the hero facing some great danger, from which he would somehow escape in the next week's episode, only to get in trouble again—and so on. The most popular serial of the 1930s followed the outer-space adventures of Flash Gordon (played by Olympic swimmer Buster Crabbe).

Next, the audience might see one or more cartoons—perhaps by Walt Disney, who had introduced Mickey Mouse to the world in 1928. Then came the feature movie—and maybe two of them if it was a "double feature." Besides the show, the price of a ticket might include "door prizes"—often kitchenware or toys—or a chance to win a more valuable prize, like a car.

By 1940 the five major studios (Fox, MGM, Paramount, RKO, and Warner Brothers) and their three smaller competitors (Columbia, United Artists, and Universal) were releasing more than 400 movies a year.

Depression era movies reflected Americans' desire for comfort and reassurance. The most popular star from 1935 through 1938, for example, was Shirley Temple, a curly-haired young girl who starred in a series of sweetly sentimental movies. And the top box-office draw at the end of the decade was Mickey Rooney, who played a "typical American teenager" in movies about life in a small town where nothing really bad ever happened.

Sound brought musicals to the screen, often featuring elaborate dance scenes. Other musicals were highlighted by singing duos (Jeanette MacDonald and Nelson Eddy) or dancing teams (Fred Astaire and Ginger Rogers). Westerns ("horse operas") were very popular, especially with children. James Cagney and Edward G. Robinson specialized in gangster roles. The Marx Brothers, W. C. Fields, and other funnymen kept America laughing. And a galaxy of stars—Betty Davis, Gary Cooper, Clark Gable, and many others—shone in sophisticated comedies, romances, and historical "costume dramas."

The year 1937 saw the release of the first full-length animated movie, *Snow White and the Seven Dwarves*. The movie took $2 million and three years to make—huge amounts of time and money by the standards of the time. Some people predicted that no one would want to see an eighty-minute "cartoon," but the movie was wildly successful.

Shirley Temple (Library of Congress)

Based on ticket sales, the biggest hit of the decade (and several decades afterward) was 1939's *Gone with the Wind*. This romantic drama was based on the best-selling novel by Margaret Mitchell about the Civil War and Reconstruction. Released by MGM, *Gone with the Wind* was the most expensive movie made up to that time, one of the first made with the new Technicolor process. The movie's premiere (first showing) in Atlanta, Georgia, was a major news story—further proof of how important movies had become in Americans' daily lives. Among the eight Academy Awards awarded the movie were Best Actress to Vivian Leigh, who played the heroine Scarlett O'Hara, and Best Supporting Actress to Hattie McDaniel, who played her mammy, or maid. It was the first time an African American had been nominated or received the award.

The Theater

Live theater thrived in the 1920s and 1930s. Broadway in New York City was to theater what Hollywood was to the movies. In the 1920s an average of 200 plays a year opened on Broadway. They ranged from the dramas of Eugene O'Neill and Maxwell Anderson to comedies like *Abie's Irish Rose*, the most popular play of the decade. Beyond Broadway were more than 2,000 theaters nationwide.

The 1920s saw the rise of the "musical," which, like jazz, would become a true American art form. The first modern musical, *Show Boat*, written by Jerome Kern and Oscar Hammerstein II, opened at Broadway's Ziegfeld Theater in December 1927. In the late 1920s and 1930s, George Gershwin wrote the songs (with lyrics from his brother Ira) for a series of sophisticated musicals, and Cole Porter's witty musical comedies, like *Anything Goes* (1934), were also big hits.

Another form of live entertainment—vaudeville—passed from the American scene during this era. Vaudeville shows featured traveling singers, slapstick comedians, and "novelty acts" ranging from weightlifters to magicians to performing animals. There were about 2,000 vaudeville theaters around the country in 1920, but as the movies gained in popularity, vaudeville started to lose its appeal. By the early 1930s the last vaudeville theaters had closed their doors. Many performers, however, made the leap to movies and radio.

Radio

If movies were cheap, radio was free—and Americans didn't even have to leave their living rooms to receive a steady stream of news, comedy, drama, sports, and music.

During the early 1920s, most radio stations broadcast only in local areas, but by 1934 four networks broadcast nationwide. The National Broadcasting Company (NBC) operated two networks, NBC Red and NBC Blue, from 1926 on. The Columbia Broadcasting System (CBS) followed in 1928, and the Mutual Broadcasting System (MBS) in 1934. The rise of national networks brought standardized programming to radio. Americans tuned into the same shows at the same time, from Maine to California.

Network programming followed a basic pattern. Mornings were a time for news and the ongoing romantic dramas that came to be called "soap operas," because soap manufacturers sponsored some of them. Adventure serials, the radio counterpart of Saturday matinee movie serials, ruled the airwaves in the afternoon, after children came home from school.

Early evenings, when the entire family was home, were filled with a mix of comedies, dramas, music, and news and commentary, often by noted journalists. Then there would be music until midnight, when most stations "signed off." The networks also broadcast live sports events, and there were lots of specialty programs, like quiz shows and "dramatizations" of plays and books.

Almost all programming was live. Comedies and dramas were performed in the studio by actors reading from scripts, with "special effects" technicians on hand to provide noises like gunshots and squealing tires. The stars of the most popular radio programs were celebrities on a level with movie stars, and celebrities from Hollywood and Broadway were often guests on the radio.

Some top bandleaders had their own programs, and programs like *Kay Kyser's Kollege of Musical Knowledge* and Saturday night's *Your Hit Parade* showcased the top popular tunes. Classical music was popular, too. NBC's symphony orchestra, conducted by Arturo Toscanini, was one of the best in the country.

Comedies were probably the most popular programs in the 1930s. Some of the best-loved comedies were performed by husband-and-wife duos. They included "Fibber McGee and Molly" (Jim and Marian Jordan), "Ozzie and Harriet" (Ozzie Nelson and Harriet Hilliard), and George Burns and Gracie Allen.

The most popular duo on the radio, however, was Amos 'n' Andy—two white men, Freeman Gosden and Charles Correll, who mimicked African Americans. While Amos 'n' Andy's humor was offensive by today's standards, the show drew 30 million listeners each weeknight during its heyday in the early 1930s.

News broadcasts made Americans feel that they were "really there" at major events. When the giant German airship Hindenburg exploded while landing in New Jersey on May 6, 1937, killing thirty-six people, broadcaster Herb Morrison's emotional report ("It burst into flames!...Oh, the humanity!") stirred emotions nationwide. (Morrison was actually recording his report rather than sending it out live, but was later broadcast.) When World War II broke out in Europe, Edward R. Murrow made dramatic broadcasts from London, with German bombs exploding in the background.

Orson Welles
(Library of Congress)

The greatest demonstration of radio's power involved fiction, not fact. On October 30, 1938, 23-year-old Orson Welles's *Mercury Theatre on the Air* broadcast a version of H.G. Wells's science-fiction story "The War or the Worlds." Many people, tuning in after Welles's introduction thought that they were hearing a news story about monsters from Mars invading America. Tens of thousands of people rushed into the streets in panic.

Publishing and the Press

Americans of this era were readers as well as radio listeners and moviegoers. Book sales shot up in the 1920s, helped by innovations like the Book of the Month Club (founded in 1926) which sent subscribers a new book every month. Many famous publishing houses, including Simon & Schuster and Random House, got their start in the 1920s. Book sales fell in the Depression, forcing publishers to find ways to cut costs. One result was the introduction of paperback books. Well-known authors of this period included F. Scott Fitzgerald, whose novel *The Great Gatsby* became an American classic. Also starting careers in this period were Ernest Hemingway and William Faulkner.

Newspaper sales boomed in the 1920s, too, with national circulation (the number of copies sold in a given year) rising from 25 million in 1920 to 40 million in 1930. A new kind of newspaper—the tabloids, which got their name from the vertical fold of the paper—emerged in the 1920s. Tabloids specialized in sensational stories of crime and scandal.

Along with newspapers, magazines flourished. In 1923, Henry Luce and Briton Hadden began publishing *Time*, the first weekly news magazine. Thirteen years later, Luce founded *Life*, which pioneered photojournalism—using photographs to tell stories. From 1925 on *The New Yorker* presented some of the best writing of the time. *Reader's Digest* first appeared in 1922. The brainchild of DeWitt Wallace, the *Digest* reprinted short versions of articles from other magazines and eventually became the nation's most popular magazine.

Through boom times and bad times, Americans had put their stamp on leisure entertainment. The coming of radio and the movies had made it possible for people across the nation to share not only the same heroes and heroines but very often the same attitudes. American popular culture was on the rise.

Chapter Nine

Fashions and Fads

The way Americans dressed and looked changed a lot between 1920 and 1940. New styles and fashions reflected changes in American society—especially where women were concerned. Fashions also reflected the economics of boom and bust. The prosperous 1920s saw the rise of flashy, showy styles, while fashions became more conservative during the serious 1930s.

America was mad about fads in the 1920s. From flagpole sitting to dance marathons, Americans developed a taste for public displays of the silly, the outrageous, and the extreme. Fads were less a part of the American scene in the 1930s, when more people were concerned with survival than with spectacle.

A group of young women (LEFT) model the latest in bathing suit fashion; some other young women dancing a popular dance called the Charleston (RIGHT) near the Capitol building in Washington, D.C. (Library of Congress)

America Changes Clothes

In the 1920s and 1930s almost all Americans wore clothes that they bought in stores or through catalogs like Montgomery Ward and Sears, Roebuck. This was a change from previous decades. For much of the nation's history, people who could afford to had their clothes specially made for them, while families that couldn't sewed or knitted most of their clothes.

Ready-made clothing began to appear around the time of the Civil War. But it took many decades before most Americans made the switch. The prosperity of the 1920s finally made it possible for many families to retire their sewing machines and buy their clothes rather than make them. So did the growth of "chain" department stores and catalog companies, which sold a wide variety of "ready to wear" clothing in standard sizes.

Also, many American women (usually the family clothes-makers) were working outside the home. They didn't have the time to make and repair clothes. After the 1920s, sewing and knitting became hobbies rather than necessary skills for most Americans. "Tailor-made" clothing would be bought mainly by the wealthy.

The switch to mass-produced clothing had important effects on American society. In earlier times, it was often easy to tell a lot about people's background from the kind and quality of clothes they wore. Poor people and those with modest incomes dressed very differently than people in the "upper class." The availability of good-quality mass-produced clothes meant that Americans looked more and more alike. It was hard to tell a clerk from an executive when they both wore the same kind of suit.

Mass-produced clothing also contributed to the growth of a truly national culture. New York still set most fashion styles, but a dress designed in the big city could now be bought in many small towns or anywhere in the country through the mail-order catalog.

Changing ideas about the body led to changes in fashion. Up until the first decades of the 20th century, both men and women considered a certain degree of plumpness to be attractive. This was because for much of the nation's history, food was relatively expensive. Looking well fed was considered a sign of prosperity, and fashions reflected this view. Clothing for both sexes was generally bulky, with many layers and much padding.

By the 1920s, however, that view had changed. Rising incomes, better diets, and a new understanding of nutrition meant that people no longer saw being plump as a sign of health and wealth. A slender body became the ideal—a view reinforced by advertising and the movies. Clothing, especially for women, became simpler, lighter, and exposed more skin.

Even though fashions changed a lot in the 1920s and 1930s, they were still fairly conservative by later standards. Jeans, short pants, t-shirts and other casual clothes were acceptable in certain settings (for men at least). But few would think of wearing clothes like these to the store, let alone to the office. Only a few pioneering women dared to wear pants in public. When actress

During the 1920s, the hemlines on women's clothing became much shorter. This dress, by the designer Elsa Schiaparelli, appeared in 1928.
(Dover Publications)

Katherine Hepburn appeared in pants (onscreen and off) in the 1930s, it caused a sensation.

Women's Fashions in the 1920s

For American women, the 1920s brought nothing less than a revolution in fashion. As the economy boomed, long-held standards of what was acceptable dress for women changed radically.

At the turn of the 20th century, skirts were long. To reveal even an ankle was considered improper by many. Hemlines (the bottom edge of a skirt) began to rise upward around World War I. By about 1920, they had risen to about knee level, or even higher— something which many older Americans found shocking. Instead of wearing a skirt and shirtwaist (blouse), as in earlier decades, many women now preferred one-piece dresses that hung straight down from the shoulders, usually without a waistline.

As outerwear changed, so did underwear. Before the new style arrived, women often wore layers of underwear. These included bulky (and often uncomfortable) "foundation garments," like corsets. By the 1920s, these had given way to much simpler and lighter undergarments.

Hair and Cosmetics

Attitudes toward other aspects of women's appearance also changed in the 1920s. Before that decade, girls wore their hair long. When they became old enough to marry, they wore their hair "up." It was pinned or tied onto their heads, often in elaborate styles.

In the 1920s a new hairstyle, "bobbed" hair, appeared. Getting a "bob" meant having one's hair cut to about mid-neck length and then curled with curling irons, or set into a "permanent wave." As with short dresses, the new style shocked many older or traditionally minded people.

The 1920s also saw large numbers of American women using "makeup"—cosmetics like lipstick, eye liner, and face powder— for the first time. In earlier decades, makeup on a woman was thought by many to be a sign of "loose morals." By the mid-1920s this attitude, too, had changed. Cosmetics became a big business practically overnight. One unfortunate side-effect of the makeup boom was that some early cosmetics used toxic chemicals, which could cause burns or scars.

The Flapper

The revolution in dress, hair, and cosmetics combined to create one of the most famous and enduring images of the 1920s—the flapper.

A flapper, in the popular image, was a young woman who wore one of the daring new dresses, with her bobbed hair under a stylish cloche hat (from the French word meaning bell, which the hat was shaped like). But the flapper image was not just a matter of fashion.

The flapper represented what people of the time thought of as the modern, independent American woman. She had a job or went to college—marriage and motherhood could wait. She danced to jazz, visited speakeasies, and dated men freely—all of which outraged those with old-fashioned ideals. She smoked cigarettes and drove a car—two things her mother probably wouldn't have dreamed of doing.

Like all such popular images, the flapper was just that—an image. Many young American women were indeed doing all of these things, but the flapper was also a creation of movies and popular books and magazines. Still, the flapper phenomenon showed that attitudes toward women's roles in society were changing.

Interestingly, no one knows the exact origin of the term flapper. It may have come from a fashion craze of the time: Galoshes (loose-fitting rubber boots worn over shoes on rainy or snowy weather) were worn unbuckled, so that they "flapped." Or it may come from the motions of popular dances like the Charleston, in which dancers flapped their arms in a way that resembled a bird flapping its wings. Or it may have been an older slang term for a young woman that became popular in the 1920s.

Fashion Fads of the 1920s

Many of the fashions of the 1920s were popularized by Hollywood. Many Americans, men and women alike, sought to dress and look like their favorite stars. Men who slicked back their hair with water or oil, for example, were nicknamed "Sheik" from the character Rudolph Valentino played in one of his most popular movies.

Other styles started on college campuses and then spread

through the nation. Long coats made of raccoon fur, for example, became almost as much a symbol of the 1920s as the flapper dress. They were good for keeping warm on a cold fall day while cheering on the school football team.

The world of sports, too, influenced fashion. Male golfers often wore plus fours—baggy shorts. (They got their name because they hung four inches below the knee.) They were worn with high, diamond-patterned Argyle socks. The style became popular off the course as well.

Men's Clothing and Appearance

Styles for men didn't change as dramatically as they did for women during the 1920s and 1930s, but the trend was toward lighter, simpler clothing.

Many businessmen and other professionals still favored the traditional three-piece suit of coat, vest, and trousers, but the two-piece suit (without a vest) became popular. In the summer, suits of white linen or a type of cotton called seersucker often replaced suits made of wool or other fabrics. A white shirt was usually worn with a suit, but in the 1920s and 1930s most men's shirts had separate collars. They were often made of celluloid (an early form of plastic), which had to be fastened to the shirt.

Except for laborers, industrial workers, and farmers, most men wore a tie to work and most other places as well. (Ties, however, weren't always "formal" wear; in the 1930s there was a craze for wildly painted or patterned ties.) Few men of the time would think of going outdoors without a hat or cap on their head. Hat styles ranged from the soft felt fedora to the wide-brimmed straw hat popular in the summer.

Most men visited a barbershop regularly and kept their hair fairly short. They were clean-shaven, too. Full beards, sideburns, and other styles of facial hair practically disappeared from the American face by the early 1920s. Thanks to the influence of Clark Gable and other movie stars, mustaches made something of a comeback in the 1930s.

The clean-shaven look wasn't just a matter of fashion. The new "safety" razor, with disposable blades, was much easier (and safer, as the name suggests) to use than the older "straight" razor. Electric razors, introduced in 1931, became very popular by the end of that decade.

Clark Gable
(Library of Congress)

Fashions in the 1930s

Just as the styles of the 1920s reflected that decade's optimism and energy, the styles of the 1930s reflected the nation's
more serious mood.

A more full-bodied look came into fashion, for both men and
women. Dresses went back to emphasizing women's curves.
Hemlines were lowered, though not to their pre-1920s levels.
Men's suits of the 1930s often had padded shoulders and a loos-
er cut.

Clothing sales fell as people simply wore their old clothes for
as long as possible and then mended them if they could. In many
families, sewing machines that had gone into the attic during the
1920s came back down in the 1930s. Children made do with
"hand-me-downs" from older brothers and sisters.

Another big development in clothing came at the end of the
1930s. This was the introduction of nylon, one of the first artificial fibers. (Artificial fibers are those made through a chemical
process, rather than coming from animal or plant sources, like
wool or cotton.)

As the hemlines of women's skirts rose, exposing more of
their legs, so did sales of stockings. Most stockings were made of
silk, which was relatively expensive and delicate, and most silk
had to be imported from Asia.

Starting in the late 1920s, the DuPont Corporation began
work on an artificial fiber that could replace silk. After investing
more than $20 million and ten years in research and testing,
DuPont introduced nylon to the world.

When nylon stockings went on sale nationwide on May 15,
1940, buyers snapped up all 4 million pairs practically within the
day. The development of nylon and other materials that followed
would have a big impact not just on clothing, but on many other
aspects of American life.

Dance Marathons

A major fad of the 1920s was endurance contests, in which
groups or individuals kept at a particular activity for as long as
they possibly could. Sometimes there was a cash prize for those
who lasted the longest.

It was also a decade when it seemed like people would do
anything to set a "world record" or otherwise bring attention to

themselves. In an era that worshipped celebrities, doing something that hadn't been done before, even something silly or dangerous, was a way "ordinary Americans" could enjoy the fame of a movie star or top athlete—if only for a little while.

The most famous kind of endurance contest was the dance marathon, in which couples competed to see who would be the last on their feet. After a few hours of swaying to the accompaniment of records or a series of bands, with only a ten or fifteen minute break every hour, the mental and physical strain became terrible.

After a few days, it usually became unbearable. Dancers dropped out, their feet burning in pain, or simply passed out in mid-step from exhaustion. There were cases of dancers suffering hallucinations and attacking their partners, or spectators. Sometimes local health officials had to step in and stop marathons before the surviving dancers became permanently injured.

Still, dance marathons remained popular well into the 1930s—because, in part, many people hit by the Depression were willing to do anything that might win them money. The longest dance marathon recorded, in Chicago, went on for 119 days. The most successful marathoners became national celebrities briefly. One, Mary "Hercules" Promitis, told reporters that she was able to keep on her feet so long because she soaked them in a mix of ice water, salt, and vinegar for weeks before a marathon.

Flagpole Sitting

Perhaps the silliest form of endurance contest was flagpole sitting. The craze began in, appropriately enough, Hollywood. In 1924, a movie stuntman named Clarence "Shipwreck" Kelly climbed up a flagpole topped with a small seat and stayed there for 13 hours and 13 minutes.

There are different accounts of why Kelly did it. He may have been paid by the theater owner to create publicity, or it maybe have been on a dare from a friend. Whatever the reason, Kelly's feat made news nationwide. Soon Americans across the country were sitting atop poles for as long they could, their only reward being beating the record, if they could, and enjoying a brief moment of celebrity.

For some unknown reason, flagpole sitting became especially popular among teenagers in Baltimore. At one point there were twenty young Baltimoreans atop poles throughout the city. One

While Shipwreck Kelly was the most famous flagpole sitter of the 1920s, other daredevils did more than sit. One of them was Joe "the Human Fly" Reynolds, who amazed crowds with his acrobatic feats. (Library of Congress)

boy, who lasted 10 days, 10 hours, 10 minutes, and 10 seconds, received a letter from the mayor, which read, in part, "[Y]our endurance...shows that the old pioneer spirit of early America is being kept alive by the youth of today."

Shipwreck Kelly remained the king of flagpole sitting. His longest stint was forty-nine days, in Atlantic City, New Jersey. All told, he spent 145 days "in the air" during the 1920s. Unlike dance marathons, flagpole sitting didn't survive into the Depression years.

Fads of the 1930s

After the stock market crash of 1929, the fad for fads began to crash, too. Flagpole sitting and similar activities seemed point-less at a time when so many Americans were out of work, hun-gry, and homeless. Almost everyone worried about what the future held for the nation, their families, and themselves.

The national passion for games that began in the boom years, however, continued during the Depression. Board games, especially, grew in popularity because they were a cheap way to pass the time.

The Monopoly craze of the 1930s, for example, was almost as widespread as the mah-jongg craze a decade earlier. In 1934, a jobless salesman named Charles Darrow in Germantown, Pennsylvania, developed a game based around buying and selling properties. (Actually, there is some controversy over the origins of Monopoly; it may have been based on an earlier game or games.)

Darrow's family and friends enjoyed the game so much that they urged him to sell it to Parker Brothers, a major game-maker. Parker Brothers rejected the game. (Among other "flaws," they felt it took too long to play.) So Darrow spent his savings to have 5,000 games manufactured. When he put them on sale in Philadelphia, they quickly sold out. Parker Brothers took another look, bought the rights to the game, and made Darrow a very rich man.

By early 1935, Parker Brothers was selling 20,000 copies of the game a week. Some people have suggested that Monopoly became so popular because it used "play money," which gave it a special quality at a time when many people had little real money in their pockets.

The big musical fad of the decade was for "novelty songs" with funny or nonsensical lyrics, like "The Three Little Fishes" (popularized by radio star Kay Kyser) and Slim Gaillard's "The Flat Foot Floogie."

College campuses were a source of fads in the 1930s, as they had been in the 1920s. In 1939, a truly bizarre fad spread across the country's campuses: swallowing live goldfish. The craze began when a Harvard freshman downed a goldfish on a dare. The story ran in a Boston newspaper, and then nationwide. Soon students were competing to see how many fish they could get—and keep—down. Colleges tried to stop the fish-swallowing, not so much out concern for the fish but because of the health dangers. The fad lasted only about a year.

The 1939 World's Fair

One event at the end of the decade captured the nation's imagination: the World's Fair in New York City.

With "The World of Tomorrow" as its theme, the fair was a huge festival which would last for a year and a half. In that time, 45 million people would visit the fair. The fairground, in Flushing Meadows in the New York City borough of Queens, sprawled over 1,200 acres. There were sixty-five miles of pathways and 300 buildings. Over it all rose two giant structures, the Trylon (a 700-foot-tall pyramid) and the Perisphere (a giant globe).

President Franklin Roosevelt opened the fair on the afternoon of April 30, 1939. In the first presidential speech broadcast on television, he announced that "All those who come to the World's Fair will find that the eyes of the United States are fixed on the future."

The seventy-five-cent admission charge (twenty-five cents for kids) gave fairgoers access to an amazing mix of education and entertainment, commerce and culture. They could visit the "national pavilions" where sixty different countries showcased their achievements, products, and culture. (Thirty-three U.S. states had pavilions as well.)

Or they could visit the exhibits contributed by more than 1,500 American companies, from U.S. Cigar to U.S. Steel. In these exhibits, fairgoers could experience the latest technology (television, color photography) and enjoy product samples (Heinz

A poster for the 1939 World's Fair. (Library of Congress)

gave out free pickles, American Telephone & Telegraph raffled off free long-distance calls). The companies that sponsored these exhibits hoped to gain publicity and boost sales of their products by participating in the fair.

In keeping with the fair's theme, some companies gave fairgoers a glimpse of what their designers thought the future would be like. General Motors, for example, sponsored the giant Futurama exhibit, one of the fair's most popular attractions. Visitors to Futurama rode on a conveyor belt through "the America of 1960," while a recording explained the wonders that awaited them in twenty years. These included airplanes made of soybean-based plastic, remote-controlled cars traveling on fourteen-lane highways, "liquid air" power sent by radio waves, and two months vacation a year.

In many ways, the World's Fair reflected how Americans felt about their country and their lives at the end of the 1930s. The Depression still continued, but there was a cautious optimism in the air. To many, it seemed like the nation had turned the corner, and that "American know-how" would indeed lead to a better future.

In 1940, the fair changed its theme from "The World of Tomorrow" to "For Peace and Freedom." Unfortunately, peace and freedom were disappearing from much of the earth. World War II began in Europe in September 1939, and over the next year many of the national pavilions shut their doors as the countries that they represented were drawn into the conflict.

By the time the fair closed in October 1940, some of the nations represented at the fair's start, like Poland and Czechoslovakia, didn't even exist anymore. They had been swallowed up by Nazi Germany and the Soviet Union.

A little over a year later, America, too, would be at war. A new era in American history would begin, and daily life for Americans would once again be transformed, as it had in the decades of boom and bust.

Bibliography

Bowen, Ezra, ed. *This Fabulous Century: Vol II, 1920–1930*. New York: Time-Life Books

_____. *This Fabulous Century: Vol III, 1930–1940*. New York: Time-Life Books

Glassman, Bruce. *The Crash of '29 and the New Deal*. Englewood Cliffs, NJ: Silver Burdett, 1986.

Green, Harvey. *The Uncertainty of Everyday Life, 1915-1945*. New York: HarperCollins Publishers, Inc., 1992.

Groner, Alex. *The History of American Business and Industry*. New York: American Heritage, 1972

McElvaine, Robert S. *The Great Depression: America, 1929–1941*. New York: Times Books, 1984

Schnurnberger, Lynn. *Let There Be Clothes: 40,000 Years of Fashion*. New York: Workman Publishing, 1991.

Sullivan, Mark. *Our Times: America at the Birth of the Twentieth Century*. New York: Scribner, 1926, 1996.

Weiss, Suzanne, ed. *The American Story: Who, What, When, Where and Why of Our Nation's Heritage*. Pleasantville, NY: Reader's Digest Association, 2000.

Index

Note: Page numbers in *italics* refer to illustrations.